Fighting Indians
in the
7th United States Cavalry

Fighting Indians
in the
7th United States Cavalry

The Recollections of a Bugler
of the Campaign against the
Nez Perce Indians
1876-77

Ami Frank Mulford

LEONAUR

Fighting Indians
in the
7th United States Cavalry
The Recollections of a Bugler
of the Campaign against the
Nez Perce Indians
1876-77
by Ami Frank Mulford

First published under the title
Fighting Indians
in the
7th United States Cavalry
Custer's Favourite Regiment

Leonaur is an imprint
of Oakpast Ltd

ISBN: 978-1-84677-960-2 (hardcover)
ISBN: 978-1-84677-959-6 (softcover)

http://www.leonaur.com

Publisher's Notes

In the interests of authenticity, the spellings, grammar and place names
used have been retained from the original editions.

The opinions of the authors represent a view of events in which he
was a participant related from his own perspective,
as such the text is relevant as an historical document.

The views expressed in this book are not necessarily
those of the publisher.

Contents

Foreword

These chronicles of stirring events were written since my discharge from the Seventh United States Cavalry, with both legs paralyzed, due to injuries received at the time of the final surrender. This regiment was made famous by that intrepid commander, General George A. Custer, and by the efficient service of its units which hastened the end of Indian hostilities in the Great Northwest.

Sitting Bull was the most resourceful war chief ever known, at the time of the Custer Massacre he led the largest and best equipped force of Indian Warriors that ever attacked United States soldiers The object of the uprising was to gain, and hold absolute possession of the lands of their ancestors, for themselves, for their children and their children's children, for all time. These hostiles, five thousand strong, were attacked by a few hundred soldiers led by Custer, June 25th, 1876, and Custer and his men were all killed. Not one was spared.

This massacre marked the beginning of the end Uncle Sam met the challenge. Hostiles bands were hunted down, and Sitting Bull was captured.

The next year Chief Joseph, realizing that Indians could not by force get or hold possession of their hunting grounds, attempted to lead a general exodus of natives into British America. Joseph had under his command, for the protection of the mass of refugees, a fighting force larger and better armed than were the soldiers under Miles, to whom he surrendered.

The careful preparation of "copy" for this book, taking the

reader from the recruiting office at Fort Leavenworth, through the Bad Lands of the North-west, picturing the actualities of my soldier life in the Big Campaign that ended Indian hostilities, has prevented the tedium of many an hour of unbearable idleness.

A. F. Mulford,
Late Trumpeter Co. M, 7th U. S. Cavalry.
Corning, N.Y., March 25, 1878.

CHAPTER ONE

Become a Soldier

In 1876, Leavenworth, Kansas, was a small, dusty, straggling attempt at a city, and although it boasted of modern government and did have a Mayor, it was way behind many smaller Eastern towns in the matter of push, population, vim, capital, and manufactories that now abound there.

Money was tight and hard to get, and although there was plenty of work, there were a great many out of employment, and to make it still worse, also were out of money—which was the case with one man I will make you acquainted with before we are through with this history.

There was a poor mud road leading from the city to Fort Leavenworth, and one mild evening a young man might have been seen trudging wearily up the hill. He soon reached the fort and inquired the way to the adjutant's office, and also asked if there was a recruiting officer at the fort?

No trouble to find them, and I soon enter the office and stand in the presence of one of Uncle Sam's own officers!

Who can describe my feelings? I can't! There was a hot streak, a cold streak, and twenty-five or thirty other streaks, all streaking it together!

I saluted in true, formal military style, (or I tried to) as I entered and found that the adjutant was really awake; I at first thought that he was asleep.

Putting on a bold front, I asked:

"Sir, can I enlist in the army?"

The officer looked at me a moment, then asked:

"Have you ever been in the service?"

"No, Sir; I have not, but I think that I should like it, if there was plenty to do," I replied.

If I had of known then a tithe of what I know now about the Regular Army, I do not think that the officers, or Uncle Sam, would have ever been troubled with business on my account.

After looking me over from head to foot, and quietly smiling, the adjutant accompanied me to the door and said to a soldier who was standing near: "Sergeant, take this man to your mess for tonight! We will examine him in the morning!"

Following the sergeant, I soon reached the men's quarters, but a short distance away. Arriving there I was shown to a wash-trough, and, after removing a coating of Kansas dirt, I was conducted to the mess room, where I was soon taking in with eyes and mouth.

It was a long room, no chairs, bare wooden tables, wooden benches to sit on; a tin plate, with a knife and fork beside each, arranged in order, are all we see on the tables.

Soldiers soon march in and seat themselves at the tables, and then in come the suppers!

What's this dish that is set before us?

Mush and molasses!

Yes, that is what stares us in the face and makes us turn pale! If there is anything on earth we hate it is mush, and now, after leaving our home in far away Corning, N.Y., to run right onto such a stack of ill-smelling mush, makes us feel like saying a bad word, but as bad words are in the mush category with us, we only say damn and present a bold front to the inevitable.

I did not intend to mention this very unwelcome ration at the start, but I have heard it said that when one has an understanding at the beginning of an engagement, he wins half the battle, so I decided to find out all about this mush question on the start, and asked:

"Sergeant, how often do you have mush in the regular army?"

"Good Lord, man don't talk so loud!" replied the sergeant. "I have been in the army for nigh onto twenty-one years, and during that time I have eaten mush on an average once a day!"

"Gee-Whiz!"

I summon up all my reserve nerve, and ask in a low but very distinct voice:

"Do they have mush on the frontier?"

"No! I heard that they once issued an order to that effect, but the men threatened to mutiny, and since that time they have not dared to mention the subject west of the Missouri river."

"What regiment is there west of the Missouri River, Sergeant?" I asked, a bright ray of hope flitting across my gizzard.

"The Seventh Cavalry! The crack Cavalry regiment of the whole army! It was Custer's old regiment, and they are equal to ten thousand cow-boys! They are terrors!"

"Sergeant, if I enlist I am going to join the Seventh Cavalry, I want no mush on my plate!"

However, my persistence prevailed, and I manage to make out a meal on bread and coffee, thanks to the sergeant, and soon after roll into a blanket and soon am dreaming. No rest for me that night.

The bugle sounds bright and early the next morning, and I hustle out to see the men as they fall in for roll-call.

After a hearty breakfast of beef stew and bread, washed down with coffee, I hang around and get a good many ideas as to the way business is conducted in one of Uncle Samuel's western forts in time of peace.

After guard mount, I accompany the sergeant to the adjutant's office, and await examination. Soon the orderly calls me into the presence of that monarch of all he surveys!

I am sharply questioned, looked over and jumped around; my eyes tested, and teeth examined in much the same manner that horse-jockeys look over a horse; height and weight taken, and then pass over to the hands of the surgeon. He trots me around for a while in the suit of clothes that I was born in, and as he finds no spavins or ringbones, I pass examination and am sworn

11

in,

Now I am a soldier, and at once draw a uniform and a sutler's check!

Now I am expected to, and must do, recruit duty, and what that duty consisted of is detailed in the following chapter. I assure you I do not put it at its worst; I try to dress it in a smile and put on its best bib, for that is bad enough to make a man regret the day he held up his right hand and swore to wade in gore for the sake of his beloved country.

Everything was new to me, and I kept both eyes and ears open, resolved to learn all there was to be known, hoping thereby to save myself many hard tasks, and harder reprimands, and unbearable lectures! I always hated a lecture of any kind.

CHAPTER TWO

Marching Orders

I soon found that life at the Recruiting Depot was not an enviable one for newly enlisted men, whether a work-shirker or one ambitious to learn by routine experience the ways and duties of a soldier. Invariably, the recruit is expected at all times to do the little jobs and the dirty work ripe old soldiers know so well how to avoid. The recruit is the one that has an extra amount of dishes to wash, of wood to cut, water to carry, potatoes to peel, slops to empty, floors to scrub, knives and forks to scour, and is very often jollied into heel-balling belts and burnishing equipment—in fact impelled to do the very work that the non-coms,—non-commissioned officers,—should do for themselves.

If there is any dirt to be shovelled, the recruits are sure to be on that particular detail.

See him now, when he gets a breathing spell. Say, don't he look like the ideal soldier; dressed in a suit of new clothes-Uncle Sam's very best—each and every garment much too large for him.

Notice that complacent, peaceful look on his face and that serene smile! He is happy now, and why should he not be happy!

He is not detailed on fatigue (work), today; he gets three feeds a day, has a pound of nigger-heel all to himself, and is not expected to know anything!

Oh, happy lot—and lots more.

But, see! Why the sudden change? His face turns pale, the smile has vanished.

Is he sick?

No!

The orderly bugler has just sounded *Fatigue Call,* and although he has been a soldier for only two days, he knows what it means; and he has also learned two other calls that he can whistle without a break. One is *Recall from Fatigue,* and the other is *Mess Call!*

He will be among the first to answer the calls last mentioned, and if not detailed to wait on table, he will try to be the first to enter the mess room, and will make the spuds and beef disappear in a manner that is truly astonishing.

It often happens that a recruit is detailed in the adjutant's office, and it is then that he is respected by all the "old hosses," as he now has—or thinks he has—a way of knowing the plans and intentions of all the officers in the whole army.

It is now his time to get even. He does so. When he comes to mess he will report that so many men are to be detailed tomorrow for extra police, on some new improvement that has struck the fancy of the commanding officer, or that the troops at the fort are soon to be sent to relieve a company on the far frontier!

Anything that will cause the most misery to the old soldiers will be meat for the adjutant's understudy for the time being,

How they will rave when they find out that they have been fooled!

But it is when recruits have accumulated to about a dozen that the life of a soldier truly begins. First comes the setting-up drill, which is very trying to one not accustomed to it. It is executed in the following manner:

The recruits are formed in a line, or as near in a line as they can be got, with head up, eyes fifteen paces to the front; then they are ordered to place their palms together, to step forward, bend over and touch the floor with the tips of the fingers, without bending the knees or in any way spoiling the rigidity of their positions!

Try it, if you think it is easy!

Other physical stunts follow.

Then comes salute, fours right and left, and so on through the whole school of the soldier.

It is fun to see them, especially if they have a big headed lance sergeant in command.

Finally marching orders come to our relief and there is no more drill for the present. Wardrobes are looked over, buttons sewed on, and all must be got ready for the trip to regimental headquarters.

There is not a bit of regret expressed by the beginners at the order to move, as they are now sure of being on an equal footing with the rest of their regiment, and free from the many petty persecutions of the old coffee-cooling Infantrymen at the Fort.

Now all citizens clothing must be disposed of, and so a pass is obtained, and away we go heel and toe to the City of Leavenworth A visit is paid to Our Uncle, the pawn broker and dealer in worn clothing, etc., and a new suit of clothes is soon exchanged for a very small sum of cash.

We take in all there is to be seen in Leavenworth, not forgetting the stuff in the bottle that cheers and dazzles, and then again climb the hill that leads to the fort, fall in at *Retreat* and again at *Tattoo*, and at *Taps* we go to bed to dream of being ridden by buffaloes, hugged by snakes, and scalped by Indians and then roasted alive, and so on until the bugle calls the weary one in the morning.

We assist in sorting and transferring an enormous amount of company property, and with an occasional wrestle with the rust on the Parrot and Rodman guns on the parade, pass away the time that intervenes between the receipt of the order to move, and the time that we do move.

CHAPTER THREE

"Inspect" the Craft!

September 23rd, 1876, orders were received at the adjutant's office for all cavalrymen at Fort Leavenworth to be sent, at once, to join their regiments.

There were thirty of us, all for the Seventh Cavalry and all young and full of what some folks would call deviltry, and I will now try and give you an account, of what we did on our way out, and also how we cooked those ducks, chewed hard-tack, and amused the people and ourselves on the long journey to the front.

We fell in on the evening of September 23rd, and after listening to a short but emphatic speech from Lieutenant Russell, the officer who was to act as our business manager on the trip, who spoke of how well he knew we would behave ourselves and what would be done to those who did not obey orders and keep quiet, we were marched to the depot, each man carrying his bundle of extra clothing and kit.

I said we were marched to the railroad depot, but now that I know what the word march, keep step, dress to the right, and the numerous other orders, not so very mildly given, mean, I must own up that we walked or straggled!

When we arrived at the depot the lieutenant told us to break-ranks,—don't know what he meant by that command, as every man of that whole thirty had a rank of his own—in fact, we must have appeared like a very rank lot of soldiers!

We spread ourselves out over the depot platform; haversacks, canteens, bundles and boots, thrown in a promiscuous heap. Then we amused ourselves for the half-hour that we had to wait for the train to arrive by asking the ticket agent and train dispatcher how far it was to Omaha, and how much it would cost to ride to the Black Hills on a Government pass! We bother him until he hardly knows which way the train was going, and until, at his request, the lieutenant ordered us to keep out of that depot!

This was a deadener on us, so, to get square with ticket agent and the lieutenant, and drive away dull care, we went down to the river's edge where we had noticed a small pleasure yacht tied up, while the excursionists were up at the fort seeing how the soldiers lived, and putting on "lugs" generally.

There was no one to guard the yacht, as undoubtedly the parties had decided that it would be perfectly safe to leave it alone, being so near the fort, and here being so many soldiers around to guard things; but they were mistaken, in the kind of soldiers that were around there at that time, or they would have left someone on the yacht to watch and pray!

It was too much for our feelings to be so near that yacht and not board her, so, accordingly we walked across the narrow stage-plank, and at once formed ourselves into a Board of Inspectors!

We were very careful not to disturb anything. But we thought there ought to be a little more steam, and accordingly opened the draft and let her zip, and she did zip!

Next we visited the cabin and examined lunch baskets and the ice-box Oh, that ice-box! We were agreeably surprised to find bottles of different calibre and colour, which, on farther investigation, were found to contain very good articles of cold tea, porter and bottled stout!

Of course the seats had to be turned over, so that the dust and the smoke would not blow on the cushions and ruin them. Pictures on the cabin walls had to be rearranged and classified. Some of the pictures looked best when hung bottom-up, or sideways.

A noise that sounded like a cannon caused us to rush to the

engine-room, where it was found that the steam was up in the forties, and still climbing for all it was worth!

It was almost train time, and as the "Inspectors" wanted to see the machinery in operation, out came the go-a-head lever. But the valve did not respond as we thought it would, and we had to hustle to get out of the way of a stream of hot water!

The next lever was pulled with better results.

You should have seen that engine start for the bank, and of course it took the boat with it!

The engine was only about three-horse power, but they were big horses, and knew when to get a gait on them. It did not make much noise, nor drive the bow of the boat into the bank very far at the first clip, but it started to dig a tunnel, and was just going out of sight towards the fort when our picket reported danger; and we left the boat to its work. It would strike and fall back for another clip, and we were having great fun watching it, when our train whistled and the gentle voice of the Lieutenant ordered us to "Fall in, and stop your damned fooling!"

The only man that literally obeyed the order to fall in tripped over a pile of bundles and he did fall in, and he knocked two other men in in so going!

The "Inspectors" were in such a such a hurry to get to their proper places in line, that they forget to f stop the engine, but they did securely tie down the whistle-cord, and we could hear that little whistle blowing fog signals long after we were out of sight of the railroad depot!

After we were rounded up in our car, and were moving along on our way towards St. Paul, we held a conflab and after due deliberation, it was unanimously decided that the yacht and engine were both dandies, and that the said excursionists were a most accommodating aggregation. Furthermore, that they had our most hearty thanks for the splendid feast prepared for our benefit, and that we would never take particular pains to find out how they admired things as they were rearranged for them during their absence to the Fort!

We also decided that the engineer would know how to stop

the engine, get the boat out of the bank, gravel out of the pump, repack the valves and piston, which we had tinkered with in order to see that they were in a proper and safe condition, and which our limited time did not allow us to replace for immediate operation.

It was also concluded that if the engineer did not stop the engine in less than a week, the boat would dig a tunnel seventeen hundred feet into the bank, and be the means of undermining the fort. It was further agreed that if ever any of us were so unfortunate as to meet the engineer, or any of his crew, we would ask if there was any reward for the arrest and conviction of the persons who indulged their inventive tendencies in this kind of experiment, and if there was, they should apply for the reward in the herein before mentioned escapade and when the said reward was secured it was to be turned into the general fund for the benefit of the grasshopper sufferers. We then transacted other business, and adjourned to meet at the call of the lieutenant.

After many narrow escapes from the guards who were stationed at the car doors we arrived at Fort Snelling, then one of the foremost recruiting stations in the department. An order was issued for us to be held there until the arrival of a large party of recruits, who were expected from St. Louis, then we were all to go forward together.

CHAPTER FOUR

On the Move

Fort Snelling, Minn., is situated on a high bluff overlooking the Missouri River, and was at that time was garrisoned by Company C, Twentieth Infantry, and I must say that they were the meanest lot of Regulars it was ever my lot to come in contact with, or to be connected with in any manner.

They kept us recruits busy from *Guard Mount* until *Retreat*, digging cellars, drawing dirt, grading, setting out trees, sawing wood, etc.

A recruit "kicked" against doing this kind of work day after day. He said to the officer in charge of the work:

"I did not enlist to farm and use the pick and shovel. I enlisted to carry a gun and march like any other soldier."

He got the gun, and with it a knapsack containing about fifty pounds of brick, which he had to carry on parade for three days, when he was glad to take a pick and shovel and resume farm work. He never after that made a "kick" although he ventured a deal of "cussing" on the side.

Company C, 20th Infantry, was at that time composed of dude soldiers, pets of dress parade officers. I never heard any of them to growl but once. That was one morning at *Guard Mount*, when the guard were marched in review, and the wife of the commanding officer, who was on the porch with their baby as the paraders passed by, told him to "Trot them around again, Pa.; it pleases the baby! Hear him laugh!"

We lonely and homesick recruits laughed in our sleeves when

we overheard expressions of indignation among the "baby entertainers" over the incident.

The old wooden block house, where hostile Reds were once most successfully *Penned*, is now used for a wood house.

The old fort is about four miles from St. Paul, and although it shows the wear and tear of age, it remains an impressive witness of the bravery of Minnesota's hardy pioneers.

Near the fort is an Indian battle ground, where many years ago the brave Penn and his old-fashioned soldiers fought and whipped three times their number of as fierce hostiles as ever trod a war path.

Favoured with passes, one rainy day, our squad visited the famous Minne-ha-ha Falls, which are about two miles from Fort Snelling. The proprietor of the only hotel at that place, much disgruntled, promptly treated us to an invitation to "Please to go back to the fort, and not do drilling on my lawns."

Such is the gratitude shown the poor, misguided men, who offer their services and their appetites to the government, for the protection of the cowboys and sutlers on the frontier!

However, we agreed to cut our visit short if the said proprietor would come across with a bite and a drink, threatening to put his establishment out of commission in case our reasonable and friendly request was not complied with.

We got the bite!

Never before did I realize how much cayenne pepper could be incorporated in a sandwich. Oh, they were hot—but they were worth all they cost. For the drink, we were given a dipper and told to all help ourselves to the water.

After climbing over the fence and interviewing the landlord's fine turnip patch, we concluded to call the accounts square, and with many thanks, and to the relief of the proprietor, we fell in for the fort, and were soon at that "Government Workhouse," as we then called it.

Somehow or other particulars of our little time at the Falls reached our commanding officer, and thereafter not one of our bunch received a pass.

We laid at the fort about ten days, and no more recruits coming, we were order forward. We were glad to get away from that place, and did not address very kindly language to members of the *Infant*-ry who were at the railroad station to see us off.

We were kindly treated by the people along the line of the railroad. At some of the stations baskets of apples and lunches were handed in through the windows of the cars—for the soldiers.

How well I remember one aged lady, who handed a pie and some cakes through a window of our car, and on our thanking her for her kindness, said: "My only son was killed in the Custer massacre." She wanted do all she could to brighten our way, for she knew we would have poor food and many hardships after we reached the hostile-infested Northwest.

As the train started on, we gave that woman as hearty cheers as ever split the air. When she bade us goodbye, she hoped the Indian war would be over before we reached the front,

It does not cost much to do these little kindly acts and this one was wonderfully helpful.

Cheers greeted us on arrival at the different places along the railroad, and we all seemed to grow bigger, and some wished we had at hand a few hostiles to practice on.

Opportunities for fun were many, and eagerly cultivated.

Many a time the train's bell-rope was given a yank, and the engineer would stop the train and come back and help the conductor locate the cause of the emergency signal. And didn't the train crew pour forth sulphurous vapours in volcanic quantities!

We ate raw salt bacon, drank cold coffee, and gnawed hardtack, and were as jolly a lot of fellows as ever filled a car.

Did you ever attempt to eat a hard-tack! If not, try to bite a piece out of an old fire-brick. I do not wonder the Government examines a man's teeth so carefully before he is enlisted; it should provide steel teeth and a file with which to sharpen them.

After a two days' ride we arrive at Fargo, a small Frontier

town on the Northern Pacific Railroad. Here we were to lay over for the night. Our car was placed on a side track near the depot.

Oh, what a feast we had that night! The lieutenant had telegraphed ahead to the proprietor of a restaurant, and on our arrival we were treated to hot coffee, soft bread and baked potatoes. Yes, and there was one thing more, and it was over a year before I tasted it again. It was butter—cow's butter, the real article, good and fresh, not a rancid double-acting foundry product.

Didn't we love that lieutenant—but we did not tell him so, as we were afraid that one of the waiter girls who had him in tow, might not like it. We all resolved to make him remember that splendid supper served aboard the car. I guess we succeeded. But girls will be girls, and shoulder straps are catching.

After supper two men were detailed to guard the car doors, and ordered not to permit a man to pass.

But, notwithstanding this precaution, every member of our party, except the guards, did go out and view the town that night. But not one of the bunch passed through a door-way of the car.

This town had had a lively experience with a large party of recruits, a few weeks before, when merchants lost large quantities of tobacco, fruits and vegetables. So on this occasion all stores were closed for the night at an early hour.

We passed a very comfortable night.

A Pullman hunting car was standing near the depot, its sides pretty well covered with the game secured that day by a party of hunters who had hired the car. During the night one of our boys brought to our car an armful of wild ducks, and reported hunting extra good in that locality.

The ducks were very carefully stowed away in the coal box of our car and artistically covered over with soft coal. Now we would have a feast, if we could only pass muster in the morning, and I do not think that there was ever a party of soldiers more anxious to leave town then we were.

Our train was to leave Fargo at 7:30 in the morning. At about

7:00 we saw the lieutenant and a couple of men coming our way. When they got to the car the lieutenant surprised us all by saying to the guard at the door:

"Did any man passed you in the night?"

"No, Sir," was the truthful reply.

The lieutenant then further astonished us by saying that there had been two dozen ducks stolen from the side of the hunting car during the night, and he then ordered all the men to open their bundles, so that the men with him could make a search for the missing game.

The bundles were opened, their contents pulled over, and not the least sign of a duck was to be found! Then the callers looked under every seat in the racks at the sides of the car, and in fact they looked in every place big enough to hold a duck, except the coal box.

After searching for nearly twenty long minutes they gave it up, and saying that they were sorry to have put us to so much bother, and expressing regret that they had even suspected us. Then one of them went to the hunting car and returned with a box of cigars, which he passed around, and left the car, to the great relief of yours truly!

Another day was spent on the road between Fargo and Bismarck, the train at times running so slow that the men could often jump off and run ahead and ask the engineer for a chew, or run ahead and try to flag the train! The reason the train went so slow was explained to me by the conductor, as being due to alkali water foaming in the boiler of the locomotive.

CHAPTER FIVE

In Camp Hancock

We arrive at Bismarck, Dakota Territory, about 8 o'clock in the evening, and are at once marched to Camp Hancock, on the main street, where we hang up for the night. We were dirty, tired and hungry, and were very glad that our journey was so near its end.

Bismarck was a thriving town of about five thousand inhabitants, notorious for its many dancehalls, gambling dens and crime holes of all kinds.

There was a large floating population of the worst characters from the East and reckless frontier toughs. Brawls and murders were frequent, mostly due to the consumption of a vicious whiskey manufactured not for from town. The buildings used for trade and commerce were of wood, cheaply knocked together, in a spread out way, high in front with a low shanty in the rear. The dwellings were mostly shacks.

Camp Hancock consisted of a row of old log huts or sheds which were built for the accommodation of the soldiers who guarded the workmen when the railroad was being built. The quarters were roomy and airy, and I guess the part we occupied had been used as a cattle-shed, as the indications pointed that way, Nevertheless we got along as well as soldiers on the march generally do, for if there is a good place available it is occupied by the officers.

After getting ourselves sorted out a little we built a fire in an old stove standing in one end of the room, and all hands set to work to undress the ducks we had secured from the hunting party, and as we had no hot water, and the ducks were cold and stiff, you can imagine what time a we had, and how the game looked when we got through. You could not tell what they were originally.

After a good deal of skirmishing one of the men found on old tin boiler. It only leaked in five places. It took us twenty minutes to stuff the holes up with old pieces of shirt, and it would sizzle. We then filled it with water and tore the ducks up as best we could and threw them in, and while one man did duty at the fire, the rest went out to forage for onions, salt, pepper, or anything that lay loose. Chagrined because we were suspected of stealing the ducks, we had resolved to have them cooked in a proper manner, even if we hid have to break our good resolutions to do it.

It was not far from 12 o'clock, midnight, when the ducks were pronounced ready and we all gathered around the boiler and then began our attack on the duckery. We had no knives and forks, nor plates, nothing but our dirty hands and fingers, but that did not worry us much, as we had the best of appetites. Two men would take a duck; and then there would be a trial of strength with one duck in the middle and a man each side, and the tough birds were dismantled. What fun, and also what a feast. It must be acknowledged that they were, to quote Puck, *Right smart, tol'ble good*, as stated at the time.

Puck, as we had named him, was a young man from Hoosierville, Hooppole County, Ill-noise, (as he pronounced it), and he was a thoroughbred, too. He got on our car at Morehead, and asked us if we could carry him through, as he was out skads. We soon had him dressed up in a suit of blue, and that uniform passed him through to Bismarck, and as he expressed it, "It was purty tol'ble done!"

It is not very often that one can beat his way on the Western roads, and it is a good recommend in this part of the county for a young man to say, in reply to the question:

"How did you get here?"

26

"I came through on my wit and muscle!"

After a hasty and scant breakfast in the morning we shoulder our packs, and start for Fort A. Lincoln, whose garrison flag could be seen on the hill, six miles distant. The lieutenant had an ambulance to ride in, and he was not decent enough to tell us to put our bundles in it, as there was plenty of room to do. Our luggage was quite heavy. Oh, what a hard march that was for so short a distance.

Only six miles across the prairie, but our bundles made it seem twenty, and a small bundle will get very heavy in a little while on such a tramp. Each of us was carrying all his worldly goods and chattels.

I suppose it was done to help toughen our muscles, as the officers are great for that, though they like to have it done by others. I thought we would never get to the fort.

After over an hour's march we arrived at the river, and there had to wait about an hour for the steam ferry boat to get up steam and come across for us.

We passed away the time while we were waiting for the boat, sitting on the muddy bank, and looking over to the Promised Land, where the camp could be plainly seen from where we were. It looked like a large village of low white huts, and the horses resembled a herd of cattle as they were grazing on the prairie below the camp. I had never before seen so many horses together—there were twelve hundred of them—and it was a scene well worthy of a place on canvass. Finally the boat came across for us, and we are soon on board, bag and baggage.

Over we go, and as soon as the boat touches the far shore we jump off and scramble up the bank as best we can. We pass though quite a crowd of Indians—Crows—who utter their guttural "*how-how*" as we pass them. On we go, passing a saw mill and sutler's store, and then turn to the left and pass along by the guard-house where General Custer once held Rain-in-the-Face, a notorious Indian guilty of killing two white men. Rain-in-the-Face was captured by Colonel Tom Custer. The Indian escaped, took part in the Little Big Horn massacre, two years later, and there in revenge cut the heart from Colonel Tom Custer, brother of the General.

We cross the parade and halt before the adjutant's office, where the lieutenant makes his report.

Our arrival at the fort is announced by the firing of one gun, and I think that if the President of the United Stated is entitled to fifty, that there should have been two hundred fired for us.

All the members of the 7th Cavalry not on duty gathered as near us as they dared to, and they seemed to act as though they feared the stars and bars, but would like to get a whack at the man who wore them! They laughed heartily at our very best attempts to stand at "attention," which command is generally given T-E-N-tion, with all the accent on the ten.

There we had to stand for nearly an hour, while the captains were selecting, or drawing cuts, to see who should have such and such a man for his collection of dogs, as that is about all they seem to think that a private soldier amounts to.

Finally, at about twelve o'clock, noon, we are all selected and assigned to the different companies; and I, for the first time, become a high-private in Company "M," 7th U. S. Regular Cavalry, and start with my first sergeant, John Ryan, to join my company at their camp on the prairie, about one-fourth of a mile below the cavalry's winter quarters.

CHAPTER SIX

Our First Meal in Camp

I was amazed and depressed, with the appearance of the camp. My patriotism went below zero as I saw how unkempt the soldiers were—unshaved, uniforms flayed and dirty; many with their hair nearly down to their collars; gaunt and hungry-looking, yet, withal, as good and jolly a lot of men as I ever met. A hearty welcome, was given us recruits; soon we were real comrades. What a difference between the real soldiers we now met, and those paper collar dudes at Fort Snelling!

Sure these Seventh Cavalry vets laugh at our blunders, and have fun at our expense, but if you are in need of anything they have you can have it for the asking; and if you want a friend who will stand by you through thick and thin, they are the boys to tie to.

I joined the company at dinner, when I for the first time take my tin cup and tin plate and follow the crowd to the cook's tent. There each applicant is supplied a plateful of baked beans, a cup of bean soup, and about one fourth of a loaf of good soft white bread. Then back to our tent we go, and eat our dinner, and it did taste good. Our morning's march had given us an appetite worthwhile, and we clean the eatables all up.

One of the men said to me,—

"Let me take your plate, and I will get you some more!"

I decline his friendly offer with thanks, and suggest that if my appetite lasts I will make a big hole in the appropriation for food. He comes back with, "It is a good plan to feed up to the limit when you get a chance, for you will need a hump like a camel, to draw on, when you get in the field."

I was assigned to one of the pup-tents, with two other men. We were soon settled and ready for callers, and the soldiers were not slow in coming to see the recruits. The vets all wanted to know what was going on in the outside world.

We tell our callers all the news we know of, and a few of the latest stories, and they meet us on equal terms, and are all are happy.

The pup-tents are made of four pieces of canvas, the sections buttoned together, with a short stake at each end and a ridge-piece. The tent, in position, is only about three feet high and four feet long. You enter at one end—that is you crawl in—and you have to stay crawled until you come out. Pup-tents are good to keep the sun off but not much protection when it rains.

While in this camp I had my first experience in mounted cavalry drill, and as I have undertaken to give you a personally conducted trip, I will give you everything just as I found it.

Back in the days when I was a farmer boy, in the township of Lindley, N.Y., I excelled as a rider of horses—and took especial delight in riding bareback.

But somehow this was different!

Indeed it was fun, fun of the funniest kind—for the spectators.

First, you are given a horse to ride bareback, and you have to jump your mount over ditches and rail fences. This is to give you confidence in your ability to ride. You do not mind it much after the first round.

Next, you are given a horse with an army saddle on, and you smile to yourself and say in your mind, that now you will show that you can ride. You soon find that you are in for a circus, and destined to be the cause of unlimited fun for the onlookers.

As you are about to mount, the stirrup straps are crossed in the saddle, and when you innocently attempt to straighten them back in their proper places,—

"Let those stirrups alone, and mount!" comes the order.

Scared out what little sense I had when I entered the camp, (for it was "Yours Most Respectfully"), I climb onto the saddle.

The horse, an old one and onto his job, puts on a horse grin and gets down to business.

As soon as I get aboard, I am ordered to,—

"Put your feet in the stirrups!"

To do so, I must draw my knees up to my chin.

Feeling like a mosquito that has been detected trying to suck blood out of a wax figure, I await what is to come next. It comes all of a sudden. The horse starts ahead in great shape and I try to keep in contact with him. The best I can do, is to meet the saddle half way every time it comes up!

Oh, what a ride! What delicious fun! I take a tumble, regain my feet, and, having the bridle rein in hand, manage to regain the saddle, and the performance continues for near an hour. I was all in, however, when ordered to dismount and "tie the horse to the line," which I do most gladly and with all possible expedition. This done, as I turned away from the head of the horse, back went its ears, and with a quick swing it lunged forward and took a not very gentle nip where saddle-blisters were already in evidence, and held on. With a jerk that almost tears away the seat of my trousers, I break away; my initiation drill is over, and I meander down the company street, tired, discouraged, mad, homesick.

Oh, that nip! Why did not that horse select some other portion of my anatomy? I had rather give an ear, that to lose a much longed-for pleasure of sitting down and giving the place the hard saddle had pounded a square deal.

The next day all recruits were drilled with their company, each recruit fully armed and equipped, and when we mounted each one painfully reminded of yesterday's exhibition performance.

When the sergeant dismisses us from drill, we greenies take a bee-line for the sutler, who has the exclusive privilege of suppling strong drink to soldiers, and we each took several doses of medicine. His treatment was so effectual, that we return to the pup tents much relieved.

CHAPTER SEVEN.

Sioux Indians Ugly

Our command laid in camp at Fort A. Lincoln for about three weeks, the men doing guard, picket and police duty by turns. I was detailed to take three men and repair the Government telegraph line, which extended from the telegraph office in the railroad station at Bismarck to the adjutant's office at the cavalry camp.

There were numerous wood choppers in the bottom lands on the Bismarck side of the river, and they were not careful whether they fell a tree across the wire or not. There were no insulators at the office, so I got a lot of ale and wine bottles and used the necks of them for insulators, and they were an ornament to the scraggy cottonwood poles we had to use. I also had a fine time stretching a new wire across the Missouri River near the camp, as the steamboat had broken the old one down with its smoke-stack. After nearly a week of hard work we got the line so we could work it all right, and then I "spelled" the regular operator at the camp.

This kind of work was finally stopped by an order that came, to the effect that the 7th Cavalry must take to the field again, and go to Standing Rock Indian Agency, and there disarm the Indians and take their ponies excepting one to each *tepee*.

Now we looked for trouble to begin, as there was a large body of the ugly Sioux at that point and they were getting the Agency Indians rather uneasy, and all were reported as getting ready to go to join Sitting Bull.

We were soon on the go, and were glad to get away from camp duty, and all looked ahead to the eighty miles that were between us and the reds as about the proper distance for an outing, and not too far from winter quarters.

As we were moving along on our third day out, the regiment was suddenly halted, and the order passed along the whole line for the men to "Dismount and tighten saddle-girths!"

The old soldiers said that now we were in for a run, as there had been a scout seen to hurry up to the commanding officer, and deliver some kind of a message, whereupon the command was at once halted. We have ten of the Crow Indian scouts with us, and as they are deadly enemies of the Sioux they did good work. They go ahead and keep a sharp lookout for hostiles and ambushes. They are enlisted, and draw the same pay and rations that a private soldier does, and for the work they do deserve more praise and pay than they ever get.

They will do more head scouting than a white scout, and are more valuable as dispatch carriers, as they are always ready, day or night, to carry dispatches to any part of the country, and will be a good many miles on their journey before a white scout thinks of getting started.

Saddle-girths were tightened, arms looked to and loaded, blankets and kits on the saddles tightened up, and all made ready for a good shaking up, as there will be no stopping to pick up anything that is dropped.

In less time than it takes to write this we are in the saddles again, and forward we move.

"Forward at a trot!" sounds the headquarters trumpet, and we prick our horses with the spurs, and trot it is.

We rise to the top of the bluff behind which we had halted, and then we can see the Indians. There are over a thousand of them!

They were less than two mile away, and were riding their ponies in a circle on the open prairie. It is a beautiful sight, especially to us poor devils who had never seen any Indians but those that stand in front of the cigar stores and held the wooden tomahawk and cigars. It is a lively scene and worth going miles to see.

"Ta-ta-ta-ta-te-ta-te-ta-te-ta-ta-a-a!" goes the trumpet, and away goes the whole command at a charge, direct for the Indians. Our sabres are drawn and slung to our wrists by the slip-knots, we hold our revolvers in hand ready for instant use, as we put the spurs to our horses and urge them ahead with a yell that echoes from bluff to bluff and through the ravines all around us.

Will they stand! They outnumber us, and we think that they mean to give us battle! On we go, horses doing their best, and still we urge them for more speed!

As we get within a mile of them the Indians suddenly turn their ponies and scamper back toward the Agency!

They are afraid to tackle us on the open prairie. That would give us too good a chance! Neither do they like the looks of those wagons that suddenly stop and turn around! Those wagons would have soon unloaded a part of their load in their ranks, and a cannon is just what they will not face!

The "wagons," as they are called by the Indians, were two Rodman and Gatling guns!

After a very lively chase of eight miles we arrived at the Agency, and the Indians gather on the prairie just below us in their village. A few rounds are fired from one of the "wagons" to show the reds what they can do, and as the balls whistle over their heads and make the dirt fly a half-mile ahead of them and their camp, they are completely cowed.

Had they charged us in a body there is no doubt but what they would have won the battle, as they were five to our one, and were all armed with rifles and revolvers, most of them having new repeating rifles, and they could handle them mounted better than our troops, as they were used to fighting in that manner

An interpreter was sent to parley with them, and to give them plainly to understand that the United States troops had been sent from Fort Rice and Fort A. Lincoln, to get their guns and ponies. That they must yield, and then they would be cared for. That the Government wanted peace, not war.

After waiting for a long time, during which the reds held a *pow-wow* among themselves and were much divided, finally a few squaws appeared bringing some old rifles and carbines. Although we knew the braves were well equipped with arms and ammunition, we could not find where they had hidden them.

We camped that night about half a mile from the Indian village—part way between their village and the agency. There I first heard their barbaric songs and music in a most disgusting setting. The reds kept us awake nearly all night, with their unearthly howlings and *cha-ce-ga* pounding—a drum similar to the rim of a cheese box, with a tightly stretched tanned head, and as unmusical as such a contrive must of necessity be.

Here for the first time I saw a war dance, as they are given in native war-councils—and the reds were not at all abashed by the presence of group of Uncle Sam's soldiers as on-lookers.

The braves were painted in the highest style of Indian art. They numbered over two hundred. Some wore bloomer-like costumes, made of light blue and bright red calico. The Indian like the Negro, wants bright colours, and they will have them too. Others wore old army shirts and moccasins, the latter being worn by all. The greater number were dressed in primitive costumes—a breech-clout, moccasins and beaver anklets, a necklace of bear claws, and a girdle. All were decorated with wing and tail feathers plucked from large birds of flight, and tin whistles were numerous. Many were nearly naked.

One brave, who was practically naked, had covered his person with an assortment of bright coloured pigments, and then, with his fingernails had scratched the colours off in odd streaks. Around his body was a belt from which hung rabbit-tails, and from his rear there hung a large bustle of eagle feathers.

The "orchestra" was composed of chosen braves, who sat on the ground, sang war songs, songs of the chase, and chanted boastingly, all the while pounding in unison on their *che-se-gas*.

Not a squaw took part in the dance. The squaws sat, or

crouched, on the ground, around the dancers, and occasionally, (while the orchestra-chorus gave way), grunted out their approval as some warrior told of his victories when on the war path, and how he had inflicted torture.

As a "curtain raiser," the braves marched into the ring and blowing whistles continuously while they jumped and shied about, twisting their bodies into every conceivable position, keeping time to the beating of the *che-ce-gas*. They lifted a foot and put down with a thud, then repeat the step with the other foot, and so on, all the time shouting "Hi-*pa! Hi-ya! Ho-ya! He-pa!*" mingled in between their dronings, boastings, and the shrill tones of whistles.

In the very centre of the ring, was a large iron kettle, containing a cooked dog. As the dance deepened in fervour, a young brave with simulated shyness as if expecting an attack by the dog, struck it with tomahawk and hunting knife, cut off some meat, dipped a hand into the stew, and giving a fierce war-whoop he tossed the bit of meat into the fire.

As the young brave finished the ceremony, shouts of approval were given by his associates while the squaws grunted again and again. The ceremony depicted the approach to, attack on, and killing of a white soldier by an Indian. The act of dipping his hand into the liquid, was to symbolize their belief that a warrior having killed a foe, who wets his hand, or hands, in the victim's blood, will be given the power to destroy all other foes.

All the braves, two or three at a time, went through the same ceremony. They were Agency fed Indians preparing to take the war-path!

Then the music and noise making ceased, and an old chief addressed the braves in their own tongue, urging united resistance to the whites. Other chiefs made like appeals.

All said and done, it was a war-meeting. We now knew what to expect!

Indian men are far better looking than Indian women. This is due to the practical enslavement of the squaws, who have to do all the hard work—cook the food, care for game, dress hides, make clothing, cut and carry wood, submit to gross indignities. The braves are, with rare exceptions, hard taskmasters.

CHAPTER EIGHT

Attempts at Escape

Only one man died at Fort Rice during the whole winter, W. Baker, of "D" Company. He died with the diphtheria, and was buried with military honours, which were conducted in the following manner:

The body was dressed in full uniform and placed in a neat coffin, and resting in a ward at the hospital, was viewed by all the men at the Post. After all take final look upon the silent face that was but a short time before wreathed in smiles, the Companies were formed in line in front of the hospital, and as the body was carried out, they presented arms, the trumpets were played and the coffin was placed on the two gun caissons which had been joined, were trimmed with black, and draped with the garrison flag—the flag that Baker had helped to unfurl so many times.

Hitched to the caissons were six horses, each with a large black plume on its head, and each led by a dismounted trooper. Then came the horse that Baker had ridden. It was saddled bridled, equipped as for a march, and his boots were tied in the stirrups with the heels to the front. This horse was led by two troopers.

Then followed the four companies of the 7th Cavalry—"A," "D," "H," "M," with carbines reversed and on foot. The line led by eight trumpeters, playing the funeral march, slowly crossed the parade, passed the guard-house; where the guard stood with arms at a present, then to the cemetery, a short distance away.

Arrived at the cemetery the troops were formed on three

sides of the grave. The burial service was then read by the post adjutant. Then the firing party fired three rounds over the open grave. Then *Taps* were sounded by one of the trumpeters, and we marched back to the fort, all much impressed by the scene we had just witnessed.

There was a great deal of trouble with the prisoners at the guard-house during the winter.

There are men in the regular army of the same class as those that keep police courts busy. As often as they get cash enough to get drunk on, such men go on a spree. These nuisances should be fired, for the good of the service.

Company "M" was afflicted with one of the worst of the species. His name was Smith. He was a New York City bum. He was in the guard-house the most of the time. He would get drunk, pick quarrels and fight on the least chance. He was the lowest of type. He and a number of chronic bums from other companies, caused guards a great deal of trouble.

When detailed for guard duty, (before I was promoted to the position of trumpeter), again and again I have received orders "Not to permit a prisoner to escape; to shoot a prisoner making such an attempt if he did not halt when ordered to!" I never had trouble with a prisoner placed in my charge.

When new to the service, on an occasion when I was detailed to guard and placed in charge of some prisoners required to chop wood some distance from camp, the officer of the day told me I must "shoot any prisoner who attempted a get-away and failed to halt when ordered to do so." For my own protection I most respectfully asked the officer to deliver the order to shoot to me in writing, and signed.

"Then," I added, "I will either bring all my prisoners in, or will furnish jobs for the surgeon and undertaker."

The officer declined to do this.

Evidently the drastic order or suggestion was not meant to be taken literally. Those on guard duty must keep within the bounds of reason.

The bums get bottles of liquor at the sutler's store. The sutler is permitted to sell intoxicants.

But to return to Smith.

On an occasion when Smith and six others were prisoners in the guard-house, every one of them in shackles, they dug out and made a temporary get-away. Smith was the leader. These men wore the shackles while digging a tunnel under a couple of the logs that, standing on end, three feet in the earth, formed the guard house walls. It was an old stockade.

The jail-break took place shortly before daybreak. It was quickly discovered. The fugitives were soon captured—all but Smith. He was not found until near night the next day, when Lieutenant Eckerson discovered Smith riding an army horse a couple of miles from camp, and brought him back.

Smith afterwards told that he had hidden for a whole day in the loft directly over the room occupied by the guard at the guard-house! How he got there was never found out. Smith would not tell.

Soon after this Smith was given a bobtail discharge and escorted out of camp by a guard of soldiers. He was told not to show himself here again.

A bobtail discharge is one with the character clause torn off, and is considered the most disgraceful one a soldier can receive.

CHAPTER NINE

Legend of Standing Rock

Early the morning after the war dance and *pow-wow* at the Indian village, *Boots and Saddles* was sounded, and in a few minutes our cavalrymen were speeding across the prairie in the direction of the ponies the Indians had refused to surrender on demand. These animals were grazing about a mile from the Indian village. The red warriors swarmed from their *tepees* and started in the direction of their ponies. Our Rodman was wheeled into position and a couple of shells, the fuses cut short, exploded but a short distance ahead of the reds. Most of the pack whirled about and speeded for their *tepees*, others stood irresolute and bewildered. The Gatling guns sang rapidly for a few seconds, and how those reds, so boastful at their war dance the night before, did "beat it!"

The pony herd was completely surrounded by the cavalry. After a brief confab between our commander and a number of chiefs, the captured ponies were driven directly to our camp, and a mounted guard placed in charge of them.

Then these reds were at our mercy. They are, as a general thing, not good fighters on foot.

We hunted for more ponies and arms, but without result. No doubt some of their best war ponies had been driven away during the night. We found one fine war pony tied down on the ground, hidden in a clump of sage brush, within a mile of the Agency.

If these so-called warriors possessed the courage to fight us, we would have had our hands full, but they were afraid of the "big heap guns." There is no doubt but the Rodman and Gatling guns kept us out of a terrible fight, and probably prevented defeat with all its accompanying horrors.

There is an Indian legend about the origin of Standing Rock. It runs about as follows:

"Long ago there was young squaw, the beauty of the tribe and loved by all, who married a young chief who was powerful as a warrior. In a battle with another tribe this chief was killed. As soon as his squaw learned of his death, she took their infant and went out on the prairie, where she stood and mourned the loss of her brave until she turned to stone!"

The story is believed by the Indians. There is the Standing Rock to prove it. The rock, as it stands, suggests the form of a squaw with a papoose slung on her back.

Indians passing that way—and many that made pilgrimages for the purpose—placed choice bits of meat, also medicine bags, at the foot of Standing Rock. They say that the spirits of the chief and his squaw come and get the offerings and take them to Happy Huntings, where they dwell in joy supreme, a place no pale face can enter.

"There are a good many Indians here, colonel," one of the officers remarked to Colonel Sturges.

"The good Indians are up there on those poles," was the colonel's reply, as the pointed towards a ridge, not far away, where the reds placed the bodies of their dead.

The body is rolled tightly in a blanket or a buffalo skin, (together with his hunting and fighting equipment if a brave), with pipe, tobacco, and medicine bags to keep evil spirits away. After the body has been prepared in this way it is placed on a scaffold of poles, elevated eight or ten feet above ground.

Should the dead be a warrior, his favourite pony is tied to one of the supporting poles, and left there to starve to death. This procedure is to provide the dead with a mount on which to ride in the hereafter.

The colonel's only son was killed in the Custer Massacre, and undoubtedly he meant, what he said.

After spending a few days at Standing Rock Agency, our command took the back trail for Fort Rice and Fort A. Lincoln, where the men were to go into winter quarters. We had about two thousand ponies taken from the Indians at the Agency, and a wagon load of old guns, sabres and revolvers, among the latter some of the old-time flint-lock variety.

Our trip thus far had been but a mild kind of an outing, and nothing happened on our return to break the dull monotony of the march.

We passed a great many Indians on the way to Agency, and they gave us a wide berth. They were anxious to reach the Agency, there to pass the winter, living and recruiting at the expense of the Government to go on the war-path in the spring.

We passed a farm where two years ago a settler had been raided by a war-party of Sioux. The settler, his wife and son were killed and scalped, the daughter was spared. The farm stock and all property the savages could use was stolen, the rest was burned.

The girl, only eleven years of age, was taken to their village, where she was compelled to marry a young warrior and do his work the same as an old squaw would. This was told by an Indian who was one of the party. He also said that the girl went crazy, recently, and with her infant in her arms and plunged into the Missouri River, mother and child being drowned.

The place where the settler, wife and son were murdered, was now the site of a substantial log cabin, surrounded by grain fields, while in front of the open door three little settlers watched the soldiers ride past.

I was told how a white man, captured by Indian warriors, was turned over to their squaws to be tortured. His clothing was all stripped from his body by the squaws, who then threw him on the ground and tied his outstretched arms and legs to firmly driven stakes. Then they stuck numerous pitch-pine splinters into his body, and set the protruding ends on fire, and then the squaws danced about the victim of their cruelty. When he would scream in agony they would spit on him and call him a coward. This torture was continued for several hours, and reached its climax when one of the squaws cut a piece of flesh from the man's thigh and thrust it into his mouth and he became a raving maniac.

Finally, tiring of the sport, they left him, yet alive and tied to the stakes, on the open prairie. There the body, or what was left of it after supplying food for prowling animals, was found a few days later and buried by a party of miners.

CHAPTER TEN

Camp Amusements

We arrived at Fort Rice about the first of December, and then had to work pretty hard, getting the forage and hay to the stables, as the corn had been left on the bank of the river during the summer by the steamers. Stables had to be repaired, and wood cut and drawn to the post for the cold weather that was sure to reach that portion of the country at an early date.

The arms captured from the Indians at Standing Rock Agency were turned over to the Ordinance Officer, and the ponies were, on their arrival at Fort A. Lincoln, placed in change of herders and started for St. Paul, where they were to be sold for the benefit of the Government.

I learned that only about 700 ponies reached St. Paul, the rest having "got lost." Uncle Sam is easy!

We passed the winter at Fort Rice, going through the following routine day after day:—

At the first streak of daylight in the morning *First Call for Reveille* would be sounded by the trumpeter of the Guard, and ten minutes later *Assembly*. Then all would fall in for the company parades, and stand at parade rest while *Assembly* was sounded by all the trumpeters.

At 6:30 *Mess Call* would announce that the scorched hash, or slumgullion, as we called it, was ready, when the men would repair to the mess room. We had potatoes, soft bread, bacon, bean soup, baked beans, and beef stews for changes, and, taken as a whole, we lived pretty well, especially before our old first sergeant, John Ryan, was discharged by reason of his term of enlistment expiring. He was the best non-com in the 7th. That is what his men thought. He was always ready to see that the men got all they were entitled to, whether there was a big company fund or not.

At 7:30, *Sick Call* would assemble those who were either sick, or wished to get rid of some duty, to the dispensary, where the surgeon would examine them and prescribe for them. Those who were able to be around were marked for "Quarters"-which meant that they were free from all duty and must stay in their quarters, and those who were very sick, were assigned to a cot in the hospital.

It frequently happened that some of the patients would have a "big head," or be too lazy to breathe freely, when they would go on the sick report, and try to pay off on the Doctor to get rid of duty, but it would not take him very long to tumble to their racket, and how his eyes would twinkle! Then what a dose they would get! Castor oil, jalop; anything to keep them moving would be administered in a good big dose! Doctor Taylor would see that it was taken, too! After the dose was down the mark was for extra duty, which meant that the man was to be given an extra amount of the work he was trying to avoid.

At 8th o'clock *Fatigue Call* would be sounded, and the men that had been detailed the evening before would start out for the work that was to be done that day. The Guards go to the guard-house, the Saddler would go to his little log hut and work at repairing halters and saddles, the sawmill men would go to the Government mill and saw lumber to be used in the different buildings, the quartermaster's men would report at the store-houses, the stable police to the stables, kitchen police to the kitchens and mess room. There was always plenty to do, but none of it hard enough to hurt a man. No soldier ever over works.

At 9 o'clock there would be *First Call for Guard Mounting*, then *Assembly of Guard Details*, and trumpeters, when the trumpeters from the different companies would gather on the parade and play a march while the guard details marched out and were received and placed in proper position on the parade by the sergeant major, when they would be reported to the adjutant as ready for inspection. The trumpeters would then play a waltz while the guard was being inspected.

The new guard would then march in review, or to the Guard House, where they would relieve the old guard and take charge of the prisoners and all property that was to be guarded. The man chosen by the adjutant as the cleanest and with the best looking equipment, would report to the commanding officer as his orderly, a position all tried to get, as an orderly did not have to stand guard nor do much of anything but buzz the hired girl in the kitchen, and eat up all the cold victuals he could find. This was called "dog robbing,"—a very suitable name!

After guard mounting, *Water and Stable Calls* would summons every man not on other duty, to the stables. Each man wore a white frock and overalls, and they were a prim-looking lot as they marched to the stables. The horses would be led to the river for water, then returned to the stables and groomed for a whole hour under the immediate direction of the first sergeant, and woe to the man who did not give his horse strict attention and a thorough going over with currycomb and brush. The shirker would have an hour or more added to his work, and there he had to stay when the rest went to their quarters and had nothing to do for almost a whole hour.

Recall would be sounded at 12 o'clock, and all work would be dropped and preparations made for dinner.

First Sergeant's Call would follow, and the first sergeants would go to the adjutant's office and get their morning reports.

Twelve-Thirty *Mess Call* would announce that dinner was ready, and the men, also, were pretty sure to be ready.

One o'clock would again be the time for *Fatigue Call*, when the different details would proceed to kill time, as they had been doing all the forenoon.

If the weather was fine, *Drill Call* would be sounded at 2:30, and then the men would put on their belts and sabres, and their longest faces, and fall in. Sometimes it would be dismounted drill, and at other times mounted, and then for a change we would have target practice, and once a great while—best of all—no drill or target practice.

At 4:00 o'clock *Recall* would announce that the time had come to cease work and drill. Then the privates would don their white suits and be ready for *Water and Stable Call*, which was sounded at 4:30, when the "Government ghosts" would again march to the stables and water and groom the horses.

At sunset, *First Call*, then *Assembly*, would be sounded, when the men would assemble on the company parades and answer to their names as they were called by the first sergeants, after which *Retreat* would be sounded by all the trumpeters, and the evening gun would be fired at the last note.

The men would now have nothing to do until 8:30, when *First Call for Tattoo* and then *Assembly*, would again call them to the parades, when the trumpeters would play *Tattoo*; then, the roll being called, they would be reported to the adjutant, and the day would close with *Taps*, sounded by the trumpeter of the Guard at exactly 9 o'clock, when all lights in the men's quarters must be extinguished.

All would then be still except the click of billiard balls in the officers' club room at the sutler's.

Each hour the guards would call out something like this: "Post Number 2, ten o'clock and all's well!"

This kind of soldiering gets very monotonous after a while, and then the boys get permission to have a stag-dance, when we have fun all by ourselves and no officers to bother us. We dance all the popular dances and take turns being the opposite sex.

We would also practice with foils, boxing gloves, and on horizontal bars, and even handle little, wicked pasteboard cards.

Every way and everything that could be thought of would be brought into use to help pass away the time, as you may rest assured that thirty-five miles from a post office, and mail only once a week, was a very lonely location.

While the days were slowly dragging along in this manner,

we had a visit from the paymaster, and we were right glad to see him, too. After paying the troops here, he was going to Standing Rock, and pay troops at that place.

I asked the captain for permission to accompany the paymaster and his escort to Standing Rock. I was given a pass for three days with permission to use my horse if I wanted to. So I joined the escort that went with the paymaster down to the Agency.

We left Fort Rice early in the morning, with the temperature thirteen degrees below zero.

My horse was all horse that day. He had got but little exercise since we went into winter quarters. He would not walk. Often he had all his feet in the air at once. My mount had a good time!

We crossed the Missouri River on the ice, and then kept along with the ambulance, that carried the paymaster and his clerk. Our ride was a long and cold one, but there were no exciting incidents in it, We did not arrive at the Agency until about dark on the same day, having marched over forty-five miles.

We put our horses out in the shed, and then started for the Catholic Indian Mission which is but a short distance from the Agency, and were very cordially received by Fathers Martin and Chrisostum, and were soon seated at a table that was just loaded with good things. We had a regular feast.

After supper we walked down to the infantry quarters and spent a very pleasant evening with the men. It was here that I learned much of the way that the Indian Agents rob the Indians and cause most of the Indians wars.

After *Tattoo* we returned to the Mission for the night, and slept in a clean warm bed that night, for the first time in nearly a year!

In the morning we attended the services in the chapel, and then visited around all day. I spent a good portion of the time at the Indian village that I helped take the ponies from in the Fall. The Indians were all very friendly.

I returned to the Mission again that night. There an Indian couple got married that night. They were as tickled as a boy with a new gun. The man was about forty and the squaw nearly as old, and they had three children to start housekeeping on.

We started on our return trip in the morning, glad that we had taken the "vacation," but sore and lame. My horse was as lively as when he left the stable at Fort Rice. *There is no place like home*, we thought when we arrived in sight of the garrison and were mighty glad to take our place beside the warm fire at Fort Rice.

CHAPTER ELEVEN

Indians at Home

Did you ever see Indians in their own homes? I will try and give you a description of them as they appeared to me, and I have no doubt but that it will be news to many who have been in the habit of reading the fiery, untamed stories that are enclosed in yellow covers.

Come with me to the prairie back of the post sutler's at Fort Rice, where there are represented three different branch tribes of Indians—Crow, Reeve and Sioux. They live in their own wild style, and visits to their villages and camps, and on all their special ceremonies, recalls to my mind the great curiosity they were to me; and with a desire to learn of them, and from them, I paid particular attention to all that happened.

In the first place, as you near the village, you observe what to you looks like a woman, with a long blanket thrown over her head, standing in front of one of the *tepees*. Holding your nose-for the stench is terrible; worse than that of a soap factory or tannery aroma. You approach as near as you think is safe, when all at once the supposed woman turns towards you, and you see that it is a man.

The dress of the sexes is very similar. With their blankets on it is almost impossible to tell them apart until they speak! You approach nearer, are greeted with a guttural "*how-how*" and respond "*how*". This is the common practice of Simon-pure savages of the Far West. Look at his dress—if it can be called dress or anything else—see what is it made of, and how it is made?

Well, it is made of three pieces of blanket, one piece for each leg, and the third and larger piece is shirt, vest and coat. The legs are made by sewing the pieces together up one side, and a strip of the same material comes up on the outside and fastens into the belt, which holds it up. The other leg is made in the same manner. Take a pair of old pants, cut the front and back out of them, and you have an extra good pair of Indian pants.

The great and only redeeming feature of this kind of pants is that they cannot be put on back side in front, as there is neither back or front in them! A necktie of rabbit-tails or beaver fur is worn around the wrists—don't know why, and I do not think that the Indian does, either, as I never found a red that could, or who would tell. His hair is long with bits of fur tied onto the end of each one of the braids, at each side of the head, and a bunch of eagle feathers stuck in the scalp-lock, a small bunch of hair braided together on the top of the head. His feet are covered with moccasins, made from the hide of the deer or buffalo, and trimmed with many different coloured beads. A large knife stuck in a rudely constructed sheath, is at his belt, always ready for instant use.

The squaws dress in much the same manner, with the one exception that they sometimes have a short skirt made of some fancy-coloured calico. They are all dirty, lousy, and lazy. I have sat and watched Indians hunt vermin on their bodies, much after the same manner that monkeys do in their cages at the circus. See her thrust her hand in under her blanket! Do not be afraid. She is not after her knife—they all carry them, too—she is after the gay and happy louse.

In this same manner I have seen white ladies in Louisiana go after the gay and festive flea!

Indians and a lice are always the closest of neighbours, and have much in common.

This is all there is of an Indian, unless it is the smell, and you would not be allowed to carry that around with you, even in an asafoetida factory.

That stringy-looking stuff hanging on those long poles is

meat that is being jerked. Help yourself to some and see how it tastes. Those long strings there are not carpet-rags, they are the inwards of a beef and will be roasted and eaten for dinner; can't you stay and take dinner with them? Take some of this, it is the very choicest delicacy that they have, and cannot be bought—it is dog meat, and very highly prized by them.

I have watched the little Indian boys, as with their bows and arrows, they hunted the blackbirds that hung around the post, and they kill a great many of them. See that little fellow there, not over three foot high and about six years old. See how he creeps along on tiptoe towards the birds. How his eyes sparkle, like a cat's that is watching a mouse; he does not make the least bit of noise as he gets nearer and nearer to his game. Now he stops and raises his bow slowly before his face, and with hardly a pause the arrow is let loose, and he gives a grunt of satisfaction as one of the birds turns over on its back. No wonder reds are the best of hunters as that is all they do.

One morning just after guard mount, a long, lank, consumptive-looking soldier entered the dispensary, holding on to his lower jaw, just as though he was afraid that it would get away from him, and groaning all the time. No use to ask what is the matter, it is evident that he is a victim of intense toothache. He not only has the toothache, but has arrived at that stage of the game when a man decides to have the blasted thing pulled, if it takes the whole top of his head off.

"Steward," he calls out, "Give me some chloroform. I have a tooth to come out, and can't stand the operation without taking something." While the steward was getting ready to do the job, Jim gazed out of the window groaning and wishing he was dead.

As he sat there he saw one of the company laundresses and the wife of an officer approach and pass each other, coming from opposite sides of the parade. Both ladies were togged in their finest fixings, were equally proud and dignified, and they passed each other with eyes front and nose up, as if each thought she owned the whole reservation, with the troops thrown in.

It was evident that both ladies just ached to look back and see what the other had on. The Laundress controlled her curiosity. Not so the other lady. She looked back, continuing her grand march as she did so, and disastrous was the result. She encountered a plebeian wheelbarrow, which had no respect of class or caste. The wheelbarrow reared up and knocked her hat off, and the lady sat down on the parade with the wheel end of the wheelbarrow on her lap. Then there was a mix-up, with striped hose much in evidence, until the lady got the barrow to lie quiet for a moment, when she sprang to her feet, recaptured her hat, and headed for her quarters.

Jim saw all this, and as the lady rose to her feet and gave the vicious wheelbarrow a parting kick, he let laughter have full sway. The toothache had disappeared.

"Steward, never mind the go-to-sleep. Haw, haw, haw! Get your forcips and yank that tooth right out quick. Hee-he, haw-haw! I'm tickled to death and the tooth is asleep. He-haw; ha-ha-haw-he-haw! Out with her before she wakes up."

The steward obeyed the order and the tooth was out before Jim got over being "tickled."

CHAPTER TWELVE

Midnight Search for Missing Men

All the fuel we had during the winter was cottonwood. When green, cottonwood will not burn even fairly well. Men are detailed to go up the river for about six miles and chop dead cottonwood trees. The wood is hauled in on army wagons. Chopping wood under such circumstances was not a desirable job, but it had to be done.

The company detail for this duty consisted of a sergeant and three choppers. They took guns, ammunition, and plenty of grub, and would camp out for a week at a time.

While our company detail was up there, there came a few days of thawing weather. The river rose rapidly, the ice went out, and soon the Missouri was over its banks, and the bottom lands under water.

Men were sent to see if the wood-choppers were safe, but could not get within a mile of the camp, and came back with a report that the camp was flooded, and not a chopper could be seen or heard, as the river covered the whole bottom, thereabouts, from bluff to bluff.

Here was a nice pickle. Something must be done. The river continued to rise. Captain French and Lieutenant Gersham, came to the company quarters and asked for volunteers to go the relief of the men at the wood camp. There were plenty of the men willing to go, as the sergeant, Paddy Ryan, was popular with the boys; and, favourite or not, our men were not the kind to refuse to do all they could to help anyone in distress.

I had been promoted to be one of the company trumpeters, a few days before, and was proud of my "Stripes and Bugle." I asked permission to go with the rescue party, and being accepted, I suggest that I take my bugle along, as I could make the missing men hear its call, and thus let the men know that help was near, even if we could not reach them.

We started from the fort about 12 o'clock at night, aboard a covered wagon drawn by four horses. It was bitter cold and getting colder. A few miles out our horses were travelling in water up to their bodies, but we keep on until we reach a side stream that was so rapid and deep that we were compelled to halt.

Here we halloed, fired guns and revolvers, and I sounded my trumpet again and again with all the power at the disposal of 165 pounds *avoirdupois*. We were within a mile of the wood choppers. We sought higher land, and, building a rousing fire near the edge of the water, waited for daylight.

As soon as it was light enough to get our bearings we made another attempt to reach the wood choppers, but deep water and the ice that had formed in still places during the night made impossible nearer approach to our objective.

The crest of the flood passed towards noon, and soon the water began to go down. Then Comrade Atkins and myself, waded on about half-a-mile and came to a wide and deep gully, where the water was swift, and which we could not cross. Here we fired a few shots and I blowed calls on my trumpet, then we returned to our army wagon, and after warming up at the open fire, our detail rode back to the fort.

We had heard nothing from the wood camp and did not know whether the men were dead or alive.

The water continued to fall during the night and the next morning Lieutenant Eckerson, of Company B, mounting a mule, rode to the cottonwoods, where he found the men all alive. Sergeant Ryan and one of the men were in a tree, the others on the roof of the log cabin. Thus, exposed to the elements, these soldiers had spent a day and a night.

All the men were victims of the low temperature. They were

taken to the hospital as soon as they were brought to the fort. The feet of one of the men were so badly frozen that it was necessary to remove all his toes. They were on the sick list for a long time, but eventually were marked "duty," and returned to their companies, ready for anything.

When Lieutenant Eckerson rode into the wood camp on the mule, Sergeant Ryan, partly delirious, began to make a verbal report of the items of Government property in his charge. The lieutenant stopped him, saying:—

"Damn the Government property! It is you men that I want to get out of this place,"

Sergeant Ryan afterwards told me, while we were celebrating his return to duty, that in the cotton-wood tree, he heard my trumpet, and it was the sweetest music that ever reached his ears.

Of course this was not fighting Indians, but I have learned that the duty of a soldier, out this way, consists more of downright work than anything else.

I had a better time after I became a trumpeter.

I now take my turn as the trumpeter of the Guard, and blow garrison calls, and I do not have to share in police duty or standing guard.

A trumpeter is the captain's hitching post, and does not get a great deal of time in which to gather moss. He is liable at any time, and especially when in the field, to be called to carry dispatches and orders, not always a pleasant task, especially in a section where scalp-hunting hostiles are numerous.

CHAPTER THIRTEEN

Comradeship With Custer

Towards spring the men began to desert, and check roll-calls were ordered. These calls were made as follows: Sometime during the night, the captain or a lieutenant would come to the company quarters and with the first sergeant, would go from bunk to bunk, (waking up those asleep), and require each man to give his name, which would be checked of as "present."

The object of this, was to prevent a man in case he deserted getting much of a start if he succeeded in getting away from the post. As soon as a man was missed, details were started in various directions and here was where the Indian scouts did their best work. They would get on the track of a deserter and follow him wherever he went, and as there is a pretty good reward for bringing in a deserter, they were very anxious to find him.

If a man did not answer when his name was called and the sergeant did not know where he was, he would be marked absent without leave, and unless he could give a good account of himself at the next roll-call to the guard-house he must go.

Our company did not lose a man all that winter, but other companies lost from one to ten men, and I never heard of a deserter being returned after he had a ten or twelve hours start.

There has been a great deal said and written about desertions from the army while on frontier service, the causes, and best remedies.

I believe the principal cause of desertions is the manner in which many of the harsh officers treat enlisted men; is due to the lack of true manhood rather than lack of knowledge. This applies to men put through the military "cracker machine" on the Hudson at West Point. Too many of the lads sent there, are spoiled and ever after disdain life's common duties, be it in the army or elsewhere. Bad officers are sure to spoil good soldiers.

As a rule an army officer does not mix with or recognize the fact that enlisted men have any rights or attributes to be respected. There is, socially, an impassable gulf between enlisted men and their officers—I qualify this broad statement by adding, "with rare exceptions." General George A. Custer was one of the rare exceptions.

Abraham Lincoln, was one of the common people. He never forgot the enduring rock of ages from which he was hewn.

Those who founded this nation, founded it on the fundamental principle, set forth in the Declaration of Independence, "that all men are created equal, that they are endowed by their Creator with certain unalienable Rights, that among these are Life, Liberty, and the pursuit of Happiness."

The aloofness of officers and harsh treatment of their men, cause a great deal of discontent, and hurts the service.

I know of commissioned officers whose evil ways are notorious. No decent man would care for their comradeship. But there as good men in the ranks of the army as there among the officers, or in any other station in life.

In my company we have one printer, one telegraph operator, a doctor, two lawyers, three professors of languages, one harness maker, four cooks and bakers, two blacksmiths, one jeweller, three school teachers, also farmers, lumbermen, peddlers, railroad men and day labourers.

CHAPTER FOURTEEN

Start from Fort Rice

Spring broke at last, when we hailed with delight the order that came for the four companies of the 7th Cavalry, then at Fort Rice, Dakota Territory, to prepare for active field service and proceed at once to Fort A. Lincoln, there to join the remainder of the regiment, and to report to General S. D. Sturges.

Those who have never been in the army, or who have never seen a regiment pack up and be in the saddle on fifteen minutes notice, know nothing of the excitement, and you might say flutter, we were in, as that order was read out to us at dress parade, at *Retreat*, on the evening of April 16th, 1877.

All had rather endure the hardships of an active campaign, and take the chances of being killed by an Indian, than remain in quarters and be abused by stiff-necked officers during the summer.

I will now give you a brief description of what had to be done in two days, for we were to start in that time. There were four companies of the Seventh at Fort Rice, A, D, H and M, each one hundred strong, and that meant that four hundred horses must be shod in that time, a night and day job work night and day by all that could work at that trade. All the saddles, bridles and halters had to be looked over, and repaired where necessary, which was quite a job for the company saddlers and their help.

Saddlebags, canteens, haversacks, *lariats*, hobbles, tin cup, picket pins, revolvers, ammunition, nosebags for horses, and all the other necessary accessories that go to make up a cavalryman's outfit, had to be got out of the storehouses and issued. Oh, no, there was not much to be done.

Each man has a box, or chest, that he keeps his personal property and kit in, and all these must be packed and placed in the company storehouse. We were not to take anything but a change of clothing, all to be carried on the saddle, and a good soldier will make his load as light as possible for his horse.

Each man bought a soft wide-rimmed felt campaign hat from the sutler, and we had to pay a good big price for the out-of-date things, too.

We were all packed and ready to move by the morning of the 18th of April, and after bidding good-bye to those who were to remain at the post during our absence, we mounted, and with all the trumpeters at the head of the column playing the tune of *The Girl I left Behind Me*, we marched through the parade and out of the post, and were at last in the field. We marched about one-fourth of a mile, and went into came for the night.

The trumpets used in the cavalry have no valves, but are nevertheless full of music, and a good player will make himself heard a long distance. We had trumpets of different keys, which we used in the fort. With these, and each man tooting when his turn came, we made pretty fair music.

As we passed out of the north gate of the garrison H Company, of the Seventeenth Infantry, passed in at the east gate. They were to guard the post during our absence, and protect the wives and children of absent officers, always provided with luxuries. "How we hate to leave the Gigger," was a remark made on all sides by the boys. The Gigger was as black a wench as ever supplied a soldier with scraps of pie and cake from a captain's pantry. She was a terror!

There were but a few women attached to our command—two laundresses to each company—and they were ladies in every sense of the word, and were respected by the common herd more than were the wives of the officers. Officers' wives in the army seem to act just as though they had a right to give orders to the privates, but they are the only ones that the rules do not recognize and provide for. When a command is on the move, there is transportation furnished for the laundresses, but their places at that time are nearly always usurped by painted dolls. Surgeon Taylor's wife was considered the only lady "across the parade." The writer of this will always remember her, with his best wishes for the prosperity of both herself and little stranger.

As an illustration of the uncertainty of coming back, I will here relate an incident that happened the morning we left the post: The companies were standing in line, ready to mount, only waiting for the "Bulldozer," Lieutenant-Colonel Elmer Otis, to bid goodbye to his family for about the dozenth time, when First Sergeant M——, of D Company, asked permission to go to his quarters and bid his wife and children a last goodbye. His request was granted, he mounted his horse and galloped to the quarters, and was there met by his wife and children. They were all in tears.

He quickly dismounts and folding his wife in his arms, said: "Mary, I have some kind of presentment which tells me that I shall not return with the boys when they come back in the Fall. I will go where duty calls me and may God take care of you and the little ones. If I fall do not forget me! Goodbye, little wife."

He kisses them all, and then mounting his horse, is soon in his position at the head of his company, and as the command moves off is seen to brush his sleeve across his eyes more than once.

His presentment, or whatever it was, came true He was shot through the lungs at the battle of Snake Creek, on the morning of Chief Joseph's surrender to General Miles.

As a general thing the officers of a regiment are very cranky after they leave good quarters, for field duty, and this occasion did not prove an exception.

Jimminey whiz; how certain officers made the man hunt tactict!

It was impossible to please them. It was first one thing and then another.

Captain French's horse—"Big-head" gave him a great deal

of trouble, and as a matter of course riled him. Oh, what a horse that was. He would go along all right for a while, and then the first thing you knew he would take it into his head to walk on the other side of the company; and, not being particular where he went, or how he got there, he would take a side carom on the company, and through he would go knocking the men out of the line, in spite of all that the captain could do to try and stop him I have seen the other officers laugh at the antics of that sorrel. The captain said that it was the only horse he ever mounted that he could not handle, but that he had to give up beat on that one.

"Old Sugar," a large bay stallion was bad enough, but "Hog" was rightly named, as he was worse than any hog I ever saw for contrariness; you can drive a hog, but you could neither drive, ride or back that horse where he did not want to go.

CHAPTER FIFTEEN

Again at Fort A. Lincoln

The first day out from Fort Rice We marched only eighteen miles, and then went into camp at about 5 o'clock at Dry Springs ravine. This place gets its name from the many little springs there, but which hardly ever contain enough water to fill a canteen. We happened to strike them at the right time, and found plenty of good water.

We pitched our tents, fed and groomed our horses and picketed them out to graze, after which I was initiated into the mystery of frying hard-tack and also lost my first ration of bacon in the operation The bacon was first fried, and then the tack was fried in the grease, after which the mess was placed in hot water, and then the tack become tender and nice. I got things rather mixed up, and set my bacon and tack on fire, and so had to skirmish for a supper.

After *Retreat, Tattoo* and *Taps*, and swapping a few stories, we crawled in our pup-tent, rather tired but otherwise feeling first rate, and were soon sleeping as sound as a man could sleep in any bed. The officers have roomy wall-tents and folding cots to help them worry though the hardships, but the common herd who have all the work to do, take up with the worst there is, and our work is increased by so many men being detailed to wait on the officers.

The camp is soon very still, no noise except that made by the horses, as they graze nearby, and the hourly call of the guards and pickets, ending with, "All's well!"

Suddenly the *Fire Call* is sounded by Chinkey Martin, trumpeter of the Guard, and we hustle out of our tents. Fire out here, and not a house or any other building within eighteen miles of us! Yes, it was a fire, and before we got through with it, it found it was the hottest and most stubborn fire we ever faced.

The prairie was on fire, and the flames were coming our way with the speed of a tornado. We hear the flames roar and crackle, in the distance, as they flash our way, fed by dead grass and dry sage-brush.

For a moment the camp is in confusion, and then *Assembly* is sounded, and every man demonstrates what discipline will do. The men fall in as coolly as if they were to parade, instead of attacking the most dangerous foe they ever encountered.

Each man was ordered to secure a section of pup-tent, and as soon as we did so, the order was given, "Right forward, four's right, double quick," and forward we go to meet the on-rush of flames. We did not stop until right at the edge of the flames. Then we whip the fire with the sections of pup-tents. Soon we begin to fall back; the heat is intense; another company rushes to our relief fighting the flames while we get a few breaths of cooler air, and then come to the relief of this company.

So it goes, turn about. Meanwhile the horses, as though they realized that there was peril for them in the prairie fire, run to the camp, crowd in among the tents, and with nostrils dilated, stand and snort. Army horses are not inclined to stampede. I think that the reason for this, is because they have horse-sense, and in a time of peril turn for protection to the men who feed and groom them. I have noticed that a cavalryman who abuses or neglects his horse, is pretty sure to be unhorsed on a march and compelled to walk.

After two hours of hard work the fire was put out where its onrush endangered the camp, and the tired men returned to their tents, or what was left of them.

While the men were working at the fire, doing their best and getting results, Colonel Otis, standing back where the air was breathable, shouted:

"Put that fire out!! Company M, move to the right!"

The colonel's orders were not kindly received. He riled some of the men, and they retorted:—

"Give that calf more rope!"

"Somebody sit on the Bulldozer!"

"I want to go home to my ma!"

Colonel Otis was so disliked by privates and company officers, that such remarks were not unusual. But when he did get after a man, his name was *Dennis*.

The prairie fire that endangered the camp was whipped out, the horses were taken back to their pasturage by details appointed to look after them, and soon all was quiet again.

An hour later, and again the *Fire Call!* The wind had changed, and the prairie fire, having turned our flank, was coming our way from another direction. We met the flames as before, and soon beat them out but got no more sleep that night.

We had met the Red Demon, in the Red Demon's own country, and won out.

We cooked and eaten our breakfasts, groomed the horse and were in the saddle at five on the march towards Fort Lincoln, which we soon could see. The fort presented a pretty picture. The old fort topped a bluff, the cavalry barracks were at the foot of the bluff, with the cavalry camp with its many white tents nearby and many horses and cattle, in separate herds, feeding on the open prairie not far away. All formed a picture that is not ever seen east of the Missouri River.

Away to the right is seen the city of Bismarck, teeming with activity; stretches of the crooked river are glimpsed at intervals.

It is Sunday, but Government orders do not pay attention to the Sabbath. On we go, over the undulating bottom land, that would make glad many a farmer in the East. No stones, no stumps or hard-heads to plow or mow around—a strip of land from two to twenty miles wide, and about eighty miles long.

We arrive at our camping place, where we join other troops, at about 2 o'clock in the afternoon.

Guidons Out, is ordered, and soon another ward is added to the famous military city on the Northwest frontier. We have "A" tents in this camp. They are roomy and comfortable.

The commissioned officers of our command are welcomed by their brother officers and entertained and soon the care of the entire camp is left to the non-coms.

We spent two days sharpening sabres, and wonder what that was for, for we did not have much faith in our present commanders as being eager to lead us on a charge against any considerable body of hostile reds.

With drills and camp work we pass away the time until April 27th. That was pay-day, with muster and inspection—we had not been paid in four months.

The Seventh Cavalry is now all together, twelve companies each one hundred strong, and we make quite a city. Out tents are pitched in the form of a triangle, with the horses *lariated* out in the rear.

We are ordered to move. On the morning of May 1st we are packed up and at the bank of the river, our company waiting its turn in crossing on steam-boats that are there for that purpose.

We are ferried across on the steamer *Far West*. From 5 o'clock in the morning until 9 at night, there is an almost unceasing sound of trumpets, and commands given by officers. After crossing the river we go into camp on the large open prairie, which stretches from the river to the city of Bismarck, nearly six miles distant.

The regiment laid in this camp one day. Many visitors from Bismarck came to the camp.

Entrenching tools were issued, a straight trowel concern, and we find them very handy to fry bacon on.

Considerable excitement was created that day, by the first appearance of one of the new Black Hills stages, or gunboats as we call them. They consist of a very heavy and large stage with a 2-pound Mountain Howitzer mounted on top. They also have twelve Winchester repeating rifles inside, with plenty of ammunition in little pockets near the windows, or rather portholes.

These stages are run form Bismarck to the Black Hills, and

despite all their arms and caution, are very frequently held up, by white as well as red devils, who rob the passengers and take valuables generally.

The Regimental band came out from the cavalry barracks, and we were treated to some first-class music, as they are one of the crack bands of the army.

You should have heard the boys cheer when the band struck up General Custer's favourite, "Garryowen." We fairly made the land tremble, when, after a few minutes rest, they played that beautiful and stirring piece, "Custer's Last Charge!" This is what should be called a mechanical piece, as the imitations of gun fire is produced by a machine which was invented for that purpose, and it is a good one, too. The air itself is lively, but when they add the sounds of carbines, rifles and trumpets, you respond in your most hearty manner.

How we wish the brave and manly Custer was with us. He was a fighter, a kind commander, and a gentleman, in every sense of the word. Custer did not want a detail at the close of a hard day's march, to put up his tent and wait on him. No, not he. "Boys make yourselves as comfortable as you can" was all he wanted at that time. He would eat his hard-tack and bacon and roll in his blanket under the nearest tree or bush, and fall asleep, but it did not take much to wake him up, and when his eyes were open he was awake all over!

"Follow me, Boys!" was his order for a charge, and who would not follow such a commander.

West Point did not spoil General Custer. He was always and ever an exemplary man, an ideal American, a true soldier.

A few days before General Custer started on the scouting expedition that resulted in the destruction of himself and comrades, he received an order from the department commander, General Terry, which said:

"It is of course impossible to give you any definite instructions in regard to this movement; and were it not impossible to do so, the department commander places too much confidence in your zeal, energy, and ability to wish to impress upon you precise orders, which might hamper your action when nearly in contact with the enemy."

Chapter Sixteen

Begin Active Campaign

May the fourth finds us packed up and in the saddle at 8 o'clock, and away we go, across the level bottom land, up a low lying hill, and are soon in the city of Bismarck, the budding Metropolis of the Far West.

How the people cheered! Everybody was out to see us pass through. They see many new faces in the Seventh—and know that many members of the old regiment are at rest in the Bad Lands of the Yellowstone.

We heard a spectator say to a companion, "If Custer was only here with them!" And if Custer had been, how the people would have cheered him!

First came the field musicians. The band had been left behind, to furnish music for the ladies.

There were twenty-five trumpeters, each mounted on a splendid black horse, the chief trumpeter excepted; he rides a large buckskin.

We play "The Girl I Left Behind Me," and "That Little German Band."

Next comes General Sturges, Regimental Commander, and Lieutenant-Colonel Otis, Commander of the First Battalion, and Major Merrill, Commander of the Second Battalion.

Then follows the twelve companies of the Seventh Cavalry, nearly every cavalryman a veteran, in columns of four's, with their company colours fluttering gaily in the breeze, and with their sabres at a present. Oh, it is a glorious sight! No circus parade ever equalled it. Cheer them, citizens; it is probably the last time you will ever have a chance! And how they do cheer! The men salute and pass along, not speaking a word.

The artillery follows close behind the men, their Rodman and Gatling guns casting a shadow over the little mountain howitzers, that rumble along by their sides; these little breech-loaders are small but will do their full share of duty before they return. The red trimmed uniforms of the artillerymen cast a strange coloured glare before your eyes, after looking at the yellow of the cavalry so long,

Ah, do not forget the wagon train, for on that depends the life of the regiment, horses and all! Here it comes! See the six-mule teams strain on the heavily loaded wagons. Sixty-eight wagons, and all loaded with hard-tack, beans, coffee, camp equipage, and oats and corn for the horses and mules. And then comes the cattle herd, that is our meat on foot, and it will all be welcome.

We pass out of main street and up over the bluffs, and are soon out of sight of all civilization.

All ride along in silence, and many have grave doubts of ever coming back. The failure of the command last summer, with the loss of so many good men on the Big Horn, make the chances of returning seem rather slim.

After marching along in this formation until about 4 o'clock in the afternoon, we halt and go into camp for the night.

Here we meet the greatest bothers that ever appear in a cavalry camp—women! Two daughters and a son of General Sturges, have been riding in an ambulance all day. So they are tired, and must have a wall tent put up for their special benefit. A detail is made to do this work, and another detail of soldiers to look after the requirements of the young ladies and the lad out on a frolic.

This compels details to delay the erection of their own shelters, cooking their suppers and giving the proper attention to their horses. It was really too bad that the young ladies got tired, but do you think that they thanked the soldiers for doing what they could to made them comfortable, Oh, no! The men do the work and the officers get the thanks.

What a difference between the conduct of such camp followers, and the wife of General Custer, who would ride all day beside the General, when on a march. And when it was time to camp for the night, she would dismount, and care for her horse-she never wanted a special detail. She was a cavalry woman.

The headquarters ladies and the lad left us next morning, in one of the ambulances under an escort, to return to Fort A. Lincoln, with nothing to do all summer but enjoy themselves. They will have an army band to provide music for numerous society functions and young officers for dancing partners.

We enjoyed a lively thunderstorm during the afternoon, and got a thorough soaking. No dry beds for the men that night.

We have no change of clothing now, so will have to get dry as best we can, and the best way is to roll up in your saddle blanket and sweat it out, all the time getting full benefit of the aroma that arises from the sweat from your horse's sides and back, as it creeps up out of the blanket.

The horses are tied to the line that is stretched between the companies, each given a quart of oats, groomed we carry our currycombs and brushes with us—and then are *lariated* out so that they may pick all the feed possible till morning, men being detailed to watch them the whole night long, by turns, otherwise a great many of them would be lost by getting tangled up in their *lariats*. Besides the *lariats* a rope about fifty feet long tied in the ring on the halter, the other end fastened in a swivel-ring on the end of a picket pin; the horses are hoppled with a strap reaching from a front to a hind foot, and buckled around the legs near the hoofs. Thus hoppled horses cannot travel as fast as a man can run, and are easily caught when they make a break.

Finally the usual routine of *Retreat*, *Tattoo* and *Taps*, having been gone through with, we lie down to sleep, but do we sleep? Not much! At about ten o'clock at night it begins to rain and blow, and we have another splendid thunder shower! Tents are blow down and go flying in every direction, and things are mixed up in great shape. We take it all in good part, only the men that

are sent to pitch the officers tents, do any growling. We catch a
few winks of sleep and are glad that it is no worse.

CHAPTER SEVENTEEN

Heavy Rains Are Active

On we go, day after day. May 7th we march through Fort Stevenson. We are halted at the post long enough for the officers to get a drink. Then on we march. Oh, what a difference will be seen in the officers after they have one drink to cut the ragged edges out of their throats.

Fort Stevenson is a small, three-company post, on the east bank of the Missouri River, and is garrisoned by three companies of the Fifth Infantry. They have about the same duties to do that we did when we were in winter quarters, but no horses to care for. Many of them said they wished they were where they would not be abused so much, but we told them they would only find that place out of the army. They said it was just like doing chores at a poor house for your board and clothes, They looked as though they lived pretty well, anyway, and I guess they found plenty of time to make love to the squaws, as there were many of these creatures around there.

We passed near Berthol Indian Agency, and camped about one mile from it. Now we see the Indians for certain, there being about five hundred of the Reeve-Sioux at Berthol.

Peaceable? Yes, if you are a big crowd and well armed. A great many of these reds came to our camp with potatoes, onions, moccasins and bead-work of different kinds, which they wanted to sell. They were not treated very well by the men and no wonder, as they are a dirty, thieving lot, and were the worst beggars I ever was.

They would approach you, and holding out a hand that would make a blacksmith blush, would say in their guttural tones:

"*How! Sar-koo-mar-koo?*" This means, how do you do, what are you going to give me? I bought a pair of buckskin leggings and moccasins of them, and they came in good after my boots had given out, as there are no worse boots made than those that are issued to the cavalry. They also had milk to sell, and our mess feasted on Mountain Stew, potatoes and bacon, and were happy. They do not raise the potatoes for their own use, but sell them to the different wagon trains almost constantly going to and from the river posts above; and also to the wheel-barrow steamboats that ply their trade on the upper Missouri and Yellowstone rivers.

May 10th my company was rear guard, and we had a picnic! We found three of the 7th Cavalrymen on the roadside, where they had fallen from their horses, and were too full to get back on their horses. They had got petty full at the Agency, and with a bottle in their pockets, had tried to keep up their spirits and the march at the same time, but had made a failure of it. When they had fallen off their horses, the captains had, with lack of humanity, ordered all the Government property taken from these men, and left them to get into camp as best they could. We placed them in one of the wagons, and that is how they came to be able to answer to their names at roll-call that night, and were saved from being reported as deserters. Oh, no, you cannot get any intoxicating liquors at the Indian Agency—unless you call for it and have the money to pay for it, at the rate of one dollar for a half-pint.

This is a very rough section of the country, being mostly bluffs and bad-lands. The prairie fires has burned the grass from nearly all the bottoms, and it was quite difficult to find a good place for our horses to graze at night. Some of the horses already begin to show the effects of the trips, and more than one cavalryman will soon have to foot it along with the wagon train, as we take no extra horses along for the men. Each officer has two for his own use, and it does not seem to make much difference to them whether the men have to walk or not.

The prairies are nearly covered with flowers, of many kinds, some of them being equal to a great many hot-house plants and as for variety there seems to be no end.

Game, such as antelope, jack-rabbits, wild ducks, prairie chickens, gophers, rattlesnakes, and buffalo-chips, is quite plentiful. We march from fifteen to twenty-five miles a day, not being able to go any faster on account of the wagon train.

On the twelfth we had quite a big scare. A scout came in and reported that Sitting Bull had crossed the river at Fort Peck, about one hundred and fifty miles above our camp, and had murdered the whole garrison, (two companies of infantry), and either carried off or burned all the government property at that place. If this is true the prospects for clasping hands across the bloody chasm are very good indeed, and when it came time to shake, (which we doubt with the present men in command), Sitting Bull will find that the Custer Avengers are right on top of the heap. We were named the Custer Avengers, while in camp near Bismarck, and hope to be able to live up to the name.

We now have an extra picket detail and guard mount, to protect against a surprise by the Indians, or red devils, as they are commonly called by the men.

I think that if the Government would hire a few farmers to go along with the command, we would not have to wait so much for the wagon train, as then the farmers would go to work and fix the roads in less time than it take the engineer corps, and it would give West Pointers plenty of time to stand and draw plans while the command crossed the bad places and pushed ahead. I shall recommend this plan in my next report to the Government!

Sunday, May 13.—Broke camp at 5 o'clock. After marching eighteen miles we camp. We now find plenty of fish, and as soon as the camp duties are done, we grab a hunk of fat bacon for bait and go fishing. Catfishes and suckers take to bacon readily, and a kind of chub was also our reward. We cook and eat a fish supper.

Another generous shower visits us during the night. Let them come. We do not catch cold.

We marched the 14th and 15th of May in about the same routine. The only thing out of the usual course that happened, was that while stepping out of an ambulance one of the hospital stewards slipped and fell, breaking a leg between the ankle and knee. The bone stuck out through the flesh and skin several inches. This man had been in three Indian battles, and did not get even a scratch, and when this accident took place he declared, "It was darn mean to use a fellow in this way."

Broke camp May 16th at 7 a. m. Marched eighteen miles and camped on the banks of Little Muddy River. This is a small creek-like stream, and gets its name from the large amount of mud and small quantity of water it contains. The only way to get a drink, here, is to take a mouthful of the mixture, and squeeze the mud out in your mouth, and swallow the water.

Two men were sunstruck today. The heat was terrible.

We were in the saddle bright and early on the morning of the 17th, In three hours we reach Fort Buford, Montana Territory. This is a large post, situated nearly opposite the point where the Yellowstone River enters the Missouri. It is garrisoned by five Infantry Companies and countless mosquitoes!

Our regiment was halted here long enough for the officers to get refreshments, when we moved to the bank of the river, and at 3 o'clock camped on a muddy bottom. No grass to speak of, considerable low brush, and too many prairie dogs holes and rattle-snakes for comfort.

Soon there was a furious thunder storm, with continuous flashes of lightning, while the water poured down. But we did not care much, it was so pleasant to have it rain so we could not drill!

My bunkie and I bought some, eggs—so we thought from the steamboat *Far West,* and the eggs proved to be too far west; that is the chicks had been picked too soon. So we had no eggs for breakfast, but we did not care much, as they only cost us fifty cents a dozen. We compounded a fairly appetizing relish of pulverized hard-tack, bacon and raisins, boiled in condensed milk.

The rumour that Mr Sitting Bull has captured Fort Peck has no foundation. However, he is reported to be about one hundred miles above this place, waiting for us. His party consists of thirteen hundred well armed warriors.

Our men are all in good spirits, and the sutler at Fort Buford is having a big trade. The demand for rattlesnake poison is brisk.

During the evening a party of infantryman came down from Fort Buford, and there was a general exchange of stories. We were inclined to believe that our visitors stretched their stories a little too much, but we did not say so.

Chapter Eighteen

General Miles Captures Reds

May 17th.—This morning it rained and the wind was so strong that it was almost impossible to keep a tent up. So we stood around in the rain, and after vain attempts to keep our fires going, we just stood and shivered, while waiting for the weather to ease up.

I had the pleasure of going to the fort with my captain, as his orderly. When we arrived there, I had the exquisite pleasure of standing out in the driving rain and serving as a "hitching post," getting wet through and through, with "Old Sugar" trying every few moments to nip an ear off as an intimation that it was time to go. But the captain staid on and on; he had a good time. The only difference between us was, that I did not enjoy myself and did get wet on the outside, while the captain did enjoy himself and did not get wet on the outside; but I will bet what little soul I have left, that in the morning my head will feel better than his does, and it will not be necessary to have my hat stretched over the top of a hard-tack box, so I can get it on.

The Second Battalion crossed the river this afternoon, to get out of the mud, and went into camp on the side of a ridge about half a mile from the Yellowstone, a short distance from the Missouri. We had packed our saddles, expecting to move, but must remain in the mud another night.

May 20th.—Another nice rainy night and the officers cross; their "A" tents were blown during the night and men had to turn out and fix them. The wood is green and covered with ice we cannot make it burn. We are to remain in this camp for the day; as it is so muddy that the teams cannot move the wagons. What a fine time this would be for an Indian surprise half the command on each side of river.

So passes another dreary any and night.

May 21st.—It is still raining. Anything dropped is pretty sure to be lost. It is astonishing how deep the mud can get and yet hold bottom. We waded through mud to the river, and had to back most of the rations and ammunition, as the mud was so deep that six mules haul a wagon that is only partly loaded. But as work is the principal part of a soldier's job, we do not mind it. After the officers' cots, tents, miscellaneous belongings and heavy chests are stowed on the boat, we lead our horses aboard and soon cross the stream. We camp near the Second Battalion, on high ground, but the rain continues.

May 22nd.—Still in camp. Mud begins to show up.

By the way, those combination frying-pans and trench-spades that Uncle Sam so kindly furnished us, free of cost, are very handy. You place the handle out straight and remove the cover, and then have a nice little plate to lay your tack and bacon on, while the part with the handle on makes a frying-pan that is large enough for all ordinary purposes. When you have finished your meal, just place any food you have left in the frying-pan part of the device, place the tin plate cover in position on top of it, and then bend the handle over the top of the plate and fasten in the catch. The bottom of the frying-pan part is made oval, shaped so it will not sit down.

We are now "at home" wherever night overtakes us, happy is clams. We go over a mile from camp to get wood. Such is our life on the Upper Missouri.

General Call was sounded bright and early, on the morning of May 23rd, by Chief Trumpeter Hardy. At 6:30 we are once more in the saddle, going on our way rejoicing. I say rejoicing, because it has stopped raining, and being up out of the mud there is a fair opportunity for our clothes to dry.

Antelope are seen on all sides. No hunting is permitted, except by company details.

An Indian scout came in today and reported that General Miles has captured about 200 more Indians, nearly all of them belonging to the Cheyenne-Sioux tribe. These he said were mostly old men, squaws and children, who let themselves be captured that they may be fed by the Government while their warriors are on the war-path. Many young braves, anxious to get a standing among their people as real warriors, are stealing away from reservations and joining Sitting Bull. They go armed with rifles and ammunition, purchased of white traders.

It begins to look as though these Indian scouts come in and report the first thing they think of, in order to make the commanding officer belief that they are doing good work.

General Miles is waiting for our Regiment to join his command, which our men are anxious to do. He is a success as an Indian Fighter. We are eager to get on the trail of Sitting Bull, and if we can force him to give battle, we will share the fate of Custer and his men, or capture the greatest war chief that ever "dug up the hatchet."

We are camped tonight on the bank of the Yellowstone, about twenty-five miles from Fort Buford. The prairie grass is about six inches high and our horses enjoy it hugely. We now have a change of diet; hard-tack, bacon and coffee for breakfast; raw bacon and tack for dinner; fried bacon and hard bread for supper. If our hunters have good luck, which they always do when Neeley is out, we feast on antelope meat. It is very tender and tastes similar to pork tenderloin but is a great deal better. The antelope is a species of small deer of a gray-brown colour. They have a patch of white on their rumps which they spread out when they run from you, and this makes them a difficult mark. Their hair is brittle.

We are told that we will strike buffalo in a day or two, if the Indians do not drive them north. We hope to live high on Indian "beef steak."

Delayed during the day by wagons getting stuck in the mud,

but nevertheless marched 25 miles.

May 24.—In the saddle at an early hour. Rained most of the night.

A lieutenant and three men arrived from the camp of General Miles, on Tongue River. They brought a despatch from General Miles to General Sturges, to hasten his advance, as the Indians were increasing their activities. Orders were at once given for the command to draw extra rations from our supply boat, the *Far West*, and then push ahead and join General Miles, making the 118 miles in four days; but our boys think this hustle will soon lose its grip, for our commanding officer does not seem to care to get in contact with the hostiles. But perhaps he is working out a plan of campaign that he keeps from his command.

General Sturges is an older officer than General Miles, and that may account for "the milk in the cocoanut"

It is enough to provoke a deacon to see so much game on every hand, and not be allowed to take a shot at it. We have strict orders not to fire a gun without orders from the commanding officer. The scouts keep his mess supplied with an abundance of game.

We march twenty-one and one-half miles and go into camp for the night. The distances marched are measured by a meter connected with a wheel on an ambulance.

May 25th.—Were in the saddle and on our way early, but were held up again and again by the wagon train. The pioneers have hard work opening a way so the wagons could get along at all. We travelled through a bottom of sage brush and prickly pears, and again camped on the Yellowstone.

The steamer *Benton* passed down the river today on her return trip from Post Number Two, on the Big Horn River. The steamer *Far West* keeps along with us, and is having a slow time of it.

"*Wash-ta-Cha-Ah*," or Good Wood, a scout, today gave me a fine quarter of antelope.

Marched twenty-five and one-fourth miles.

May 26th.—After a soaking rain in the morning we are off, and at night camp on the bank of Glendive Creek. Another rumour brought in by one of our scouts, is to the effect that 500 Indians have left Standing Rock Indian Agency and are on their way to join the hostiles north of us.

Nineteen miles forward today. There is a supply camp here at Glendive, guarded by two companies of infantry. This is one of the prettiest spots I have yet seen, and on the side of one of the bluffs, glistening in the sun, is a large mass of what I am told is mica, of good quality.

Day after day we march over wild country, where roaming bands of hostiles watch our movements but keep beyond reach. They have keen judgment as to the distance our rifles will carry.

CHAPTER NINETEEN

Indians Capture Mail

Sunday, but only in name. There was an alarm last night, given by the mounted pickets. We turned out in short order, and were all ready for the fun to begin, when we found that a small party of reds had tried to creep up on a picket, and on being discovered had fired their guns and taken to the bluffs.

No use to try to capture them. They know every rod of these bad-lands, and easily get away.

Broke camp early in the morning and made a still march. Our route led us through bad-lands over bluffs, across alkali bottoms where the dust from the grass made breathing a torture and caused eyes to smart and swell; but through it we must go. The horses are thirsty and it is difficult to keep them from drinking the alkali water. This water is extremely repulsive, in taste and smell. It stands in small ponds and the salty vapours that rise settle on the grass and sage bush all about, forming a coating similar to frost. It gives great trouble to Indians and whites. Marched 29 miles and camped on Sunday Creek.

May 28th.—We start early on our seemingly endless march. There was an interesting incident, when a young antelope appeared along the line of march, and ran ahead and some of the officers gave chase. Though only about four months old it gave the horses a lively race for over a mile, when an officer rode up beside it and bending over grasped it by the back and lifted it aboard his saddle. After giving the little fellow a good ride, it was placed on the ground, and followed after for some distance, when it turned aside.

We saw three large elk today, but the captain could not get near enough for a shot. They were big fellows and had amazingly large spreads of antlers.

We also caught sight of a small herd of buffalo. After a hard but short run our detail succeeded in bringing one of them to the ground. We had "Indian beef" for supper.

Another despatch came in from General Miles for our command to hurry up. We would be compelled to make long detours to accommodate our wagons but by putting in more hours could gain one day in three. We are only fifty miles from Tongue River Cantonment, General Miles's headquarters, and one forced march would land us there in a day; but our commander does not seem inclined to "hurry up!" It is common talk among the men, that General Sturges is cranky because he is under orders to report with his command to General Miles, a younger officer.

A man of Troop E was sunstruck today. He was brought in in the ambulance.

Passed the United States Mail this afternoon. It was on the way to Fort Buford. The mail train consisted of a white man, with long hair, well armed, and two ponies; he rode one and the other carried the mail on a pack-saddle. Think of this for bravery! For sixty dollars per month this man travels alone in a hostile country with the valuable mail. These mail carriers are the best scouts in the country and hardly ever fail to deliver their mail safely and promptly. Once in a while a mail carrier is killed and scalped by reds, who take all he has, even his clothes.

Thirty-five Indian warriors were seen today ahead of the command. They were spies from Sitting Bull's camp, and watched us closely, and then went to a distant bluff and started signal fires, to let their head-quarters know our location, our strength, and the direction in which we were moving. These signal fires can be seen a great distance, and as manipulated by the Indians are an efficient means of communication

Struck a good camping place at 5 o'clock in the afternoon

and up went our tents for the night. Our march was 18½ miles, to get ten. Wood and alkali water abundant.

May 29th.—Today General Sturges received word from General Miles, to the effect that Sturges is to wait for Miles, who will join him in a day. We then expect to take pack mules and push ahead, with fair prospects of getting in contact with hostiles.

Camped in a large bottom, surrounded by high bluffs, with plenty of wood and good water, and grass abundant. Our horses are in bad shape. They require plenty of good feed and potable water. A mount has a heavy load to carry—as it is all a man can do to throw the packed saddle on the horse's back, and to this burden is added the weight of a man.

The following morning my company was ordered out on a scout. We took one day's rations, and were soon in the saddle, with rain falling quite hard. We went straight away some twenty-five miles, and then took a circle to the left and returned to camp, not having seen a hostile that day. Our route was through some of the worst country I ever saw; over bottoms covered with prickly pears, cactus and sage; through bad-lands; over and along bluffs where it seemed that a horse could not keep on its feet, but at any moment would tumble to the gullies below; along steep ridges that looked as though the earth while in a molten state had boiled over.

We passed through places where masses of volcanic formation suggested the wreckage of large stone buildings, torn to pieces, the ruins of long ages gone. Many of the blocks were as square as though chiselled out, and not a few of them lay in about the same shapes that sticks of a woodpile would, if piled up straight and nice, and then tipped over.

Our Indian scout, "John-Climb-the-Bluff" as we call him, was right at home here. He would hurry and climb to the top of a cliff, and if the route was one we could get through he would signal for us to come on; otherwise he would wave for us to stop while he searched for an opening, and when he found one would beckon us on. It was a day of most interesting adventure.

Generally speaking, this is a bad country. It is a proper place for Indians. Here the reds have game in abundance. But it has minerals, restricted farming and range possibilities, and other possibilities that lure the whites. No decent white man would be content to live the life of a savage. A white who is a hunter, is good for nothing else. But, as things have gone since the frontier line began its westward sweep from the Atlantic seaboard, three centuries ago, whites will continue their drive, until the last frontier has been wiped out. And out here in the Bad-Lands the desperate aborigines are making their final stand!

Here's a Wild West Classic, of unknown origin, that is handed about the camp, keenly enjoyed by the men, who are mailing copies "to the home folks:"

Dakota's Wail.
To the west of Minnesota,
And among the treacherous Sioux,
There you will find Dakota,
Where the skies are never blue!
So, stranger, come and find a home—
If bad fortune you'd pursue—
In this glorious land, of blizzards grand,
Where they fasten clothes on with glue!

It is not a mazy woodland
Where the alligator crawls,
But some level and more Bad Land,
With poor streams and waterfalls,
Where Uncle Samuel gives a farm
To everyone that calls—
A farm of land, great big Bad Land,
Where the water always falls!

Upon the plains the buffalo
No longer can be found,
And in the streams thin fishes grow
That scarcely weigh a pound;
From mountains of snow rivers flow,

That in the Springtime rile;
And impelled by steam, boats ply the stream,
For fifty cents per mile.

Here nature plies her fingers
To portray her darkest page;
Here no happy boyhood lingers,
The lads are bent with age!
Here nature sends her fiercest winds,
And with sickness you engage;
A land of stealth, there is no wealth—
Here poverty is all the rage!

In Dakota there are mountains
Up near Montana's line,
Where poor water springs in fountains,
And hills will not grow pine.
And, Oh! 'tis here the pioneer
His pouch with no grub fills—
Black, stern and bold, where the rich are sold,
Is this land of Black Hills!

CHAPTER TWENTY

A Birthday Party

May 31st.—Very rainy and blustering in the early morning, followed by clearing, and then a light fall of snow, and then sunshine. Had to skirmish for fuel; the supply was scant. But little stir in camp all day. Men laid around rolled up in blankets to keep warm.

June 1st.—Still waiting for General Miles. We are to move to a better camping place, to get wood and water and to give the horses better grazing.

We are now short of rations, but expect a supply today. The teams have been gone two days, and as they did not have far to go, there is uneasiness on their account. If they or stuck in the mud, or have been captured by Indians, we will become desperate. Two of our non-coms were placed under arrest today for going on a hunt for something to eat. They were released and returned to duty a few hours later. Discipline must be maintained! With game so abundant and nearby, it is a shame that hunting details are not sent out. The men plan to help themselves, if the food shortage is not soon relieved. That would be a serious reflection on our commanding officer.

Company M went out today on another scout. We got a thorough soaking before we returned to camp. Sitting Bull is not inclined to take the initiative, but various commands of our forces are ready to close in on his massed warriors at the first opportunity. He is a crafty red-skin.

June 2nd.—A splendid morning; the sun shone out bright and hot.

Moved camp about two miles to get grazing for the horses. A scout came in at sundown, bringing mail for our regiment. It was received with delight. I opened a late paper (three months late), and saw eggs quoted at 12c a dozen. We would gladly give 12c each for reasonably fresh eggs.

The latest in regard to the command of General Miles, is that he is on the way and may be expected at any time, but it is not believed possible for him to reach us soon, because mud is now so deep that teams could not get through with necessary supplies.

There are no hostiles in this section now, but they are reported to be gathering in large numbers near the Blue Grass Mountains and Milk River, about sixty miles from our camp.

June 4th—Sunday again. Weather fine. Two scouts just rode in, their ponies covered with foam. They reported a party of Sioux warriors crossing the river three miles above our camp. General Sturges has sent a wagon train, under strong guard, to the river, to bring in supplies left there by a steamer.

We hang pretty close to camp, while scouting parties are out to find out what the Sioux are doing; our scouts report that there are no hostiles anywhere near us.

On the afternoon of the 5th we had mounted drill; but to my mind our horses need food and rest more that such exercise; many of them are so worn down as to be unfit for service.

Sergeant M——, of Company M, was Right Principal Guard for Colonel Otis, and on coming to battalion, right front into line, got way out in front of the battalion, into the position that belonged to the colonel. If there is anything that the colonel dotes on, it is his position; that must not be encroached on. So the expected happened. He exploded!

"What are you doing here in front of the battalion?" he shouted at the startled sergeant.

"I was trying to get in position and you crowded me out!" the sergeant replied, saluting.

"Where are you from; where do you belong?" the angry colonel asked.

"From Boston, Sir," replied the rattled sergeant.

"I wish you had staid there!" said the colonel as he rode off to find another Right Principal Guide.

A very cold evening. As I was trumpeter of the Guard, I spent the night on the side of a bluff, nearly a mile from camp, with the pickets, so I would be at hand, if we were approached by hostiles during the night, and could sound the *General Alarm* and arouse the camp.

Two Indian scouts came in and reported Indian trails and a camp of reds a few miles out. Company H was routed out and at once started on a tour of inspection, with orders to bring in all Indians they can find. Captain Benteen started out, delighted with the order. He is not the man to run away from an opportunity to have a little fun with the reds.

A team started under guard, for Tongue River, after tobacco. Most of the men have been without this ration for three days, and are getting desperate. This morning a member of Company B, tobacco hungry, dropped in at Headquarters, and asked General Sturges for a chew! The general complied and asked the man how long he had been out of the weed. Emboldened by his success, the man replied:

"Over a week, and if I do not get a supply soon I will skin out and go where I can get it."

He was soon under guard.

I have seen men nearly crazy due to their unsatisfied longing for tobacco. It is often sold for ten dollars a pound by men who win large quantities of it at poker.

June 6th.—We had battalion drill this forenoon, which was immediately followed by rain.

June 7th.—More rain! Continued in camp.

On the 8th of June we broke camp early in the morning, and were happy to be once more on the go. It is much more soul satisfying to march through constantly changing scenery, than to stay in camp and drill. We had gone a short distance, when the command was suddenly halted and ordered to camp. This action is much like that of a man who is not firmly decided whether to do a job of work; he begins, then suddenly throws aside his tools and sits down.

Luck was with us this time. We soon had our tents pitched, on the banks of Cherry Creek. This is an ideal camping place, as far as grass and water are concerned, but we have to carry wood about a mile.

General Sturges today issued an order for all the trumpeters to practice calls, marches and quicksteps one hour each day, when in camp.

Snowstorm this evening.

June 9th.—We had drill by companies in the forenoon and battalion drill in the afternoon. Just as the drill was over, it was our luck to be treated to a nice shower, so instead of being able to take a nap, we curl up in our pup-tents and roll from side to side, trying to dodge the rain that seeps through the thin canvas. These tents are just heavy enough to shed the sun, but are not good for anything else, unless it is good to whip a grass fire with.

June 10th.—Sunday, as usual, no religious service.

June 11.—In camp. During the afternoon and evening Colonel Otis gave a birthday party, entertaining the commissioned officers. The festivities were held in a hospital wall tent pitched near head-quarters, with all the company guidons stuck in the ground around it.

Chapter Twenty-One

Mounted Indians Race
Into Our Camp

June 13.—Broke camp at 9 o'clock and marched a single mile. Camped and drilled until the horses were nearly tired out.

One of our Indian scouts in telling a companion about the cars he had seen in Bismarck, described them as "Heap wagon; no hoss!" and that is about what this expedition has amounted to so far, "Heap march; no fight!"

Company B ordered out on a scout towards Deadwood, where hostiles are reported on the rampage. They took rations for thirty days.

June 14th, rained most of the day. One company was sent on a scout to Big Horn river.

After battalion drill on the 15th, just after we got our horses "on the line," there was a cry of "Indians" from the pickets, and we saw way off on the prairie mounted men coming our way, with their horses on the run. We were quickly formed in line in front of the officers, and thought that there was a job of real work cut out for us. On they came, past the pickets and right up to the command. They were Indians for sure, but they were our own scouts. They had been out on a scout and were racing their vigorous and well-kept ponies back to camp.

Didn't we shout at the discovery! And didn't the picket catch it for giving the alarm. But the picket had obeyed orders to give an alarm on the approach of a body of Indians.

June 15th, 1877—A fine day but rather cool. We have Battalion drill and target practice in the afternoon. Mounted target practice is fascinating. The target is made from pieces of hardtack boxes shaped to resemble a man standing erect. The company is formed in a right front into line, and then the men file off from the right of the line, with horses at a walk. They do not stop their horses, but as they pass the target they try to see how many bullets they can put through the tack man, firing from the shoulder; that means having the muzzle of your revolver held on a level with the shoulder, and then firing as soon as the arm is extended.

As soon as the men get so that they can hit the target with their horses on a walk, at thirty paces from it, they go at a trot, then lope, and at last as fast as their horses can run. It is very exciting, both to man and beast, and it is considered good shooting to hit a target and load and hit it again, in a distance of not more than forty yards, and your horse on a dead run all the time.

After drilling and taking care of our horses, the men loaf around, sleep, tell stories, or sing. Here I must tell you of our singers, as they are called, Henry Humer, Robert McNeil, "Whitey" Cane, and "Boots", the *basso profundo*! They are as good a lot of singers as can be found in the army.

Colonel Otis often asks them to sing his favourite for him, "Mother, Kiss Me In My Dreams." They will sing it for him, but they know he hates to hear "Susan Jane" the "One-Horse Open Shay" and other pieces of that kind, and generally end it up with one or the other of them, You can just bet it makes us smile, and we encore our songsters.

June 17th.—A hot, sultry day, and in the after-noon the grasshoppers came in great numbers. They were so thick that they formed a cloud between the earth and the sun, similar to an eclipse, for about an hour. As the wind died out they settled to the ground, completely covering everything. They chewed holes in our tents, blanket, overcoats, etc., and one of the men lost thirty rounds of ammunition, and when questioned as to what had become of it, he said that the grasshoppers had eaten it, brass shells and all.

They were the largest I ever saw, some of them being over two inches in length.

The pests are called Egyptian locusts.

The man who carries the mail between Fort Buford and Tongue River, came into camp this morning on foot, minus mail and outfit. He reported that he had been surprised by a party of hostiles as he was eating and his ponies were resting, and had saved himself by skulking through the sage bushes; the reds had taken the two ponies, the mail, and express packages, and disappeared in great haste.

Company D, was immediately ordered to take one day's rations, go to the place where the robbery took place, pick up the trail of the thieves and capture or kill them and recover the mail. The mail carrier was taken along, as also a number of Indian scouts.

We are again short of rations.

Company I was ordered to report at Tongue River Post, in light marching order, which means no tents, no extra clothing, no supplies. Company I got off this morning.

There are indications of a general move on the hostiles. There was mounted regimental drill and target practice in the afternoon.

June 19.—Weather fine. In the saddle at 7:30, go five miles and camp on Cedar Creek. This stream gets its name from a small grove of cedar trees on its bank.

Company D returned from their scout after the mail thieves, and reported following the trail until they overtook them, when the Indians scattered. Our men did not recover anything.

General Call sounded bright and early the morning of June 20th. We move forward 18 miles and camp. Had a lively time with rattlesnakes as we began camp work, but a free use of sabres soon cleaned them out. Prickly pears and cactus are so thick that we are given orders to camp at will, which we did. The result was a general mix-up.

Two men on picket duty fired their guns at jack-rabbits, and were ordered brought in. They were taken before Colonel Otis, who lectured them and placed them in charge of the guard, with orders that the culprits be required to walk during marches for a whole week. One of the offenders said: "Got two rabbits and are to have a vacation for a whole week!"

June 21st.—Broke camp at 6 o'clock, and after marching fifteen miles camp in a very fair place, with good feed for the horses. We have now butchered the last of our cattle, and will for a time be without fresh meat, as we are out of the way of deer and antelope.

Some of the men found what they termed lamb's quarters, a tender and pleasant tasting edible weed, which we gathered and cooked as we would dandelion greens. They made excellent food. We also found Indian wild onions in abundance—which went very well with the greens. We go a mile for water; the only fuel obtainable is "buffalo chips."

June 22.—March four miles and camp on the banks of Big Sunday Creek, only three and one-half miles from Tongue River Cantonment. Miles City can be seen in the distance; a large assemblage of tents, log houses and rough board huts, squatting on the V shaped lands formed by the junction of the Tongue and the Yellowstone Rivers. There are groups of tall cottonwood trees nearby.

We see near the landing stacks of forage for the cavalry, and the camp of General Miles's renowned Eleventh Cavalry-composed of members of the Fifth Infantry mounted on ponies captured from the Indians. A quaint, but useful, little ferry boat, guided from side to side of the river by wires so adjusted that the current sup-plies the propelling power, keeps on the move. On the flat land beyond Miles City are large stacks of prairie grass, which will be hauled across the river as soon as a sufficiently strong ice-bridge has been constructed by Jack Frost.

This is Miles City, as seen from a distance. It is a rough place, full of saloons, gambling hells, dance halls and brothels.

Our present camp is the thirtieth we have occupied since

April 21st, and during the interval we have marched one thousand and three hundred miles!

It is rumoured that we are to go from here to Milk Mountains, and there we will find plenty of big game. These rumours are always interesting.

Chapter Twenty-Two

At Last Ready to Close in on Reds

June 22nd, 1877.—Rattlesnakes are very thick here, but no
one has been bitten yet and all very careful not to be. While lying down on the ground today, to take a nap, Captain French
heard a slight rustle in the sage bush near his head, and he was
not long in getting up either. On investigating with sabre he
found a fine rattler, and soon transferred its spirit to the happy
hunting grounds.

A wagon train with fifty wagons came in today from Tongue
River. They brought forage and rations. The teamsters reported
General Miles as fixing up for a big campaign.

Ordered out on another scout, today, and while out met a
party of one hundred and fifty Indians. They said they were out
on a hunt, by permission of General Miles, and as they had one
of Miles's scouts with them, we let them proceed on their way.
The scout who was with them, as I was then informed, is a
half-bread, who shot and killed a man at Cheyenne Agency in
1876, but he has never been arrested or even examined on the
subject, and goes and comes at will, being considered a hard case
and owing to his readiness with a gun, is considered a bad man
to tackle.

He is reported to have married one of Sitting Bull's daughters, and has been employed as a scout by General Miles all
summer. He looks like a dirty, lazy loafer, but must be a good
scout, or else General Miles would not have him around. He is
also said to be one of the scouts who refused to go into the last

battle with Custer

On the morning of June 23rd, I went up on one of the bluffs, on a prospecting tour for moss agates. There are splendid ones on the higher ridges. I found a great many that would compare favourably with any I ever saw in rings that cost as high as fifty dollars. They are of different shades, shapes and sizes, and many of them have inside what looks like the shadow of a bush.

The headquarters team went to the post today, and came back with some nice new and heavy pup-tents for the officers. This looks like business. Rained in the afternoon, and mail for our regiment arrived from Tongue River.

June 24th.—No moving orders yet. Bought a dozen eggs. They turned out to be condensed chickens, but the sutler charged the small sum of one dollar and twenty-five cents for them just the same. So our surplus is again reduced, without any personal benefit, It seemed rather hard to pay such prices, but you must do it, The men in power will give one man the exclusive privilege of accompanying the regiment, and the sutler charges the men what he has a mind to. Of course he does not charge the officers as much as he does the men, and that makes it all right in that quarter. Great pains are taken to keep that wagon at the head of the train.

The question arises, "But why do soldiers buy of the sutler if he charges such excessive prices?" Well, we all admit that we ought to pass up the sutler, but if a man is sick and tired of tack and bacon, and has only short allowances of that part of the time, and has a chance to get anything different, even if it takes a whole month's salary to procure one square meal, he will make the venture. A man will pay any price for a meal rather than endure the pangs of extreme hunger. And if a soldier has not got the ready cash, he can easily get a sutler's check which will buy just as much as cash, and the amount is deducted from the soldier's pay by the paymaster. Sutler's should not be allowed to issue such checks, and should be compelled to rely on their resources to keep up with a command.

June 25th, 1877.—This the anniversary of the Custer Massacre on the Little Big Horn. The brave General and his entire command, sent out by General Terry, department commander, on a scout, were trapped by Sitting Bull, whose fighting force was twelve times as large. Now Setting Bull must know his days are numbered.

This is a rainy day. Had inspection and mounted drill, with sabre and revolver practice. In the afternoon it was very warm. We can see and hear the steamboats on the Missouri and Yellowstone rivers, so do not consider we are entirely out of the world. There are thirty-eight different steamers on the up-per Missouri this Summer.

June 27th,—A fine day. Drill! Drill! Drill! Some of the horses are about all in.

Saw some unusually large meteors during the evening. One of them was in sight for fully one minute, lighting up the heavens for miles around, and then it disappeared as suddenly as it came.

CHAPTER TWENTY-THREE

General Miles Takes Command

The sun came out very hot the morning of July 1st, but thunder soon began to rumble, and large and densely black clouds gathered in the distance, and came direct for our camp. Tent pins were driven deeper and preparations made to make the best defence possible against the wind and rain. The storm was furious. Tents flew around in the air. The best we could do was to lie close to the ground. We were afraid that the wind would blow that away too. Occasionally we could hear hard words, as the wind would take some man's hat or blanket and go dancing over the prairie with it. We let things amuse themselves, and when the storm was over gathered what we could find and were soon house-keeping once more, but with parts of our houses missing. Needless to say we got soaking wet most of the officers included.

A trumpeter "got rattled," when the storm having passed over, he was ordered to sound *Stable Call*, and instead sounded *General Call*—which is the signal to take down tents, pack saddles and get ready to move. The men got busy, but a moment later the trumpeter "came out of it" and restored things to their proper order by sounding first *Recall* and then *Stable Call*. But didn't that trumpeter catch it at headquarters, where he was immediately wanted. He was given a reprimand, and that closed the incident. As an excuse, he said to the adjutant, "There must have been sand in my trumpet!"

The adjutant said, "You need more sand in your gizzard!"

July 2nd, 1877.—The only thing out of the usual routine of camp duties that transpired today, was the detailing of cavalry-men to act as artillerymen.

July 3rd.—Ordered to break camp at 3 o'clock in the morning. Something is going to happen!

A despatch came in, saying that hostiles had appeared in force near Glendive Creek, and that an attack was feared. Help was asked for, and two companies of the Second Cavalry, which were then in camp at Tongue River, and five pieces of artillery were put on the steamboat Kansas, and away they went as fast as steam and current could take them. They have orders to join us in three days, to march north, if it is not necessary for them to stay at Glendive. More rain in the evening.

July 4th,—And hurrah for everybody!

Broke camp at two o'clock. No one but General Miles knows where we are going, and he is not the kind of a man to tell.

We made a still march of about twenty-four miles and then went into camp. General Miles joined us in the evening, with a wagon train of seventy wagons, and one hundred pack mules. There seems to already be a different look on the way things are to go. We now have a man at the head who is not afraid of his shadow, and who we think will make others hump themselves to keep up with the procession.

General Miles, although a young man, seems to be possessed of fine judgement, and does not put on as much style when at work, as a clerk in the adjutant's tent. He is as brave as was General Custer, though we miss in him that dash that caused General Custer's death. He wants to see where he is going, but when he sees he goes. He is called "Buffalo Soldier" by the Indians, and they say that no bullet can hurt him. We hope that none ever will.

The ground was covered with a thin coat of snow this morning, but it turned out to be very warm during the day. Camped on Custer Creek. Slight fall of snow in the evening.

On the 5th of July, we broke camp at five o'clock in the

morning. Company M was rear guard today, and we had lots of fun helping the wagons out of the mud, and over bad portions of the road.

Thermometer at 90 degrees in the shade of the ambulance; no water along the route only what we can get out of the mud holes.

Our command now consists of nine companies of the 7th Cavalry; two companies of the 2nd Cavalry; five companies of the 5th Infantry (which are mounted on captured Indian ponies), one heavy parrot gun and one small breech-loading mountain howitzer.

We have seventy wagons, two hundred pack mules, thirty Indian scouts, and four white scouts. In the commissary department they have twenty California and Texas packers, who pack, unpack, and take care of the mules and attend to the cattle herd, which now numbers about seventy head but will soon be reduced to nothing if we do not get where there are more buffalo.

After marching over twenty-eight miles we camped on the banks of High Creek. This creek gets its name from its high banks, which rise for hundreds of feet on either side.

July 6th we were in the saddle at five o'clock, and headed for Idaho Territory, glad to be rid of the dull monotony of camp life, but sorry that our horses are not in better order, as they have nearly had the hides drilled off from them.

It is a grand sight to look back and see the long columns of troops and wagons crawling over the prairie, the pack mules all following the gray horse with the bell on; and to see the big stacks of hard-tack boxes weave from side to side as the mules plod steadily along. The gray horse is called the "Bell-horse;" and the mules will follow it wherever it goes.

Watch that mule that is slyly getting out of the line; do you know what he is going to do? I do, and so does that packer who is coming, with his horse on a run. When a mule gets tired, or lazy, whichever it is, or both together, he will step out of the line, and if not watched very close, will lie down, and as the load is so heavy that he can't get up with it on, they have to be unpacked in order to get them up.

See him get down; there he goes, flat on his side!

Now the mule must be unpacked, whipped to his feet, and repacked when he gets back on all fours, and the whip will be a propelling power to make him hustle and catch up with the rest. It would not do to let them all stop when one goes down as they would all be apt to lie down, and it would detain the whole command for near an hour waiting for the mules to be unpacked, got on their feet and repacked and in marching order again

A mule is no fool, and a fool is not a mule; you can bet on that every time.

The following conversation between Colonel Otis and Major Merrill was overheard today by an orderly:

"Major, what name do you think the men use when they refer to me?"

"Don't know," the major replied.

"Bulldozer!" said the colonel in an angry tone.

"That is nothing," said the major, "they refer to me as Four-Eyed-Son-of-a-Gun!"

And so it goes, "the men" have a nickname for each officer-some complimentary, some otherwise.

CHAPTER TWENTY-FOUR

A Thrilling Adventure

We passed over the battlefield of 1874, where General Stanley and his command were so badly cut up by Sioux Indians. Bones were strewn on the ground quite thick. Here is the skeleton of a horse and close to it the skeleton of a man, the bare and bleached bones glistening in the sunlight, and the whitened skull looking grinningly up at us as we ride past. Near these bones we notice a dozen or more empty cartridge shells, sure proof that the soldier had died in the line of duty.

"Will our bones ever lie and bleach in such a place?" we wonder as we go on—to we know not what!

We now ride over a beautiful table land, flat and smooth as a barn floor. It forms a point made by the Yellowstone River and High Creek, where they join; then through bad-lands, cut up by deep ravines and gulches. Not a spear of grass or a bit of cactus or other growth relieves the eye. This is a land of desolation. We enter a deep ravine, and along the bottom we go, rock walls rise thirty, sixty, in places a hundred feet above our heads on either side. What a place for an ambuscade! But our scouts are ahead and it is safe to follow them.

Cutting sand and fine dust strike our faces, fill our eyes and make breathing difficult. Look, there are massive rocks ahead that block our way; no, we take a sharp turn to the right, and emerge from desolation directly into paradise! The finest, smoothest, largest meadow I ever saw is right before me—a meadow where a scythe has never been swung. The rich grass brushes the legs of the cavalrymen as they ride through it.

Halt!—sounds the trumpet.

Dismount!—it sounds again, and we get off our horses, remove the bits from their mouths and let them eat and be happy while they can. We are to wait here until the wagon train catches up with us.

General Miles is half a mile ahead of us with his scouts. He is signalling. What does that mean?

Indians!

The trumpet sounds *To Horse!*—and we quickly put the bits in our horses' mouths, and are ready.

Mount!—goes the trumpet, and we mount. There is no confusion, no misunderstanding the tones of the trumpet, for it is in the hands of Chief Trumpeter Hardy himself.

Forward!—sounds the trumpet again, and forward we go. We make for that bluff where we can see General Miles.

When we had gone a quarter of a mile, we saw someone leave the bluff and ride full speed to intercept Trumpeter Hardy. The two meet, Trumpeter Hardy bends over in the saddle to receive an order, sent by General Miles, and then as he straightens up there is a bright flash in the sunlight. He has in hand the copper bugle he carried when he was with Custer during the Civil War. See! He raises it to his lips and the tones of the bugle sound out clear and strong. What melody! But what is the order?

Companies Right Into Line!—and putting ourselves into that position in an instant, we ride forward.

Gallop!—is the next call. At last! Aha, this is something like it! Just what we had heard about but had given up all hopes of taking part in.

A trumpeter of each company is with his captain, and another stays by the first sergeant of the company. It is the duty of these company trumpeters to tell what the calls mean and to repeat them.

How our travel-worn horses do pull out, each doing its best.

Deploy Skirmishers, By the Right and Left Flank!—is the next call sounded, and the six companies of the Seventh Cavalry take their positions twenty yards apart, with horses on a gallop.

Charge!—commands the bugle of Chief Trumpeter Hardy. Twelve Company Trumpeters repeat this call, and on we go as fast as we can make our horses travel. We make the top of the bluff, and, whew! about two miles distant are about two score mounted Indian braves, and there may be several thousand more behind that other bluff. On we rush—but will the reds stand? No, they are off! See them lash their ponies! Hear them yell! Uphill and down we keep up the chase, but get no nearer the fugitives. Our horses are flecked with foam and many of them begin to lag. The wagon train and pack mules are out of sight.

We reach the top of a ridge, and on the flat land below, quietly resting on the bank of Cherry Creek, are our savages-those two score Indians we have been trying so hard to catch. We have been chasing our own scouts, friendly Cheyennes and Crows, who had that morning been sent on ahead to scout for hostiles.

Recall was sounded, and *Rally by Companies* follows. We are soon in proper trim. Word was then passed along, that General Miles wishing to see now the Seventh Cavalry would respond in an emergency had instructed the scouts to make the fake run, and they most successfully complied with his orders.

We went into camp. The wagon train and pack mules came in late.

CHAPTER TWENTY-FIVE

Jim's Strange Feast

Broke camp on the morning of July 7th at six o'clock, marched about ten miles and went into camp on the battlefield where a part of General Miles's command had a tussle with a body of Sitting Bull's warriors last summer, and whipped twice their own number. There are thousands of old *tepee* poles and wooden pins lying on the ground, where they were abandoned by the reds. The *tepee* poles are from ten to twenty feet long, straight and smooth, one end of most of them having been worn to a sharp point, due to being dragged on the ground. When moving their villages, the Indians fasten one end of two or more *tepee* poles on the sides of a pony and permit the other end to drag. On the back of pony as well as on the dragging *tepee* poles unduly heavy burdens are carried.

Buffalo bones are scattered all about this former site of an Indian village. There are hundreds of deer and buffalo hides staked down to the ground, which shows that the squaws were engaged in their tanning processes when surprised by the soldiers. The hides were all hard and wrinkled, and were good for nothing.

We explored the old village pretty thoroughly.

Mainly little bags of paints and charms were found as also an old carbine, an old flint-lock pistol, a few axe-helves with the letters "U. S. Q. M. D." branded on them, part of a coffee-mill the drawer of which contained a quantity of beads and herbs done up in bits of rags, and tied with pieces of sinew.

Several axes and the axe-helves, with the coffee-mill, were

relics of the Custer Massacre. A horse-brush was found by one of the men, that still bore upon its back the following inscription, cut in with a knife:

C. B., Co. F., 7th Cav., 1873.

This brush had belonged to a sergeant in that company, who was killed in the Indian campaign, of 1873.

My company was detailed for picket duty tonight and had just got the pickets posted, when around came an order for the First Battalion to be ready to start on a five day's scout at 5 o'clock in the morning. We were at once relieved from picket duty, and drew extra ammunition, and enough hard-tack and bacon to keep us good and salty for six days. We did not get but little sleep all night long. Now that General Miles has left us, we expect to do nothing but fool around from camp to camp, and drill what little life our horses have out of them.

Broke camp the morning of July 8th at 5 o'clock, and taking a pretty fresh Indian trail, followed it until about 5 o'clock in the afternoon, then halted for the night. Have to govern our marches now so as to keep behind Indians that may be on the war-path, and so that we will have water at the camps. March thirty miles. We have no extra clothing but overcoats, and many of the men have not got that much, as they have thrown their overcoats away in order to lighten the load of their horse.

General Miles left us to go to Glendive, taking Company E as an escort.

We pass abandoned *tepee* poles and other Indian belongings in large quantities, indicating that the reds ahead of us are in a hurry.

July 9th.—Broke camp at 5 o'clock and follow the Indian trail. Marched over rough country. Saw numerous antelope. Pass three dead ponies, and two dead Indians. The bodies of the Indians had been placed on poles. It is probable that the ponies had been sacrificed that their owners might enter the Happy Hunting grounds in due and ancient form.

Pawnee Tom, a half-breed scout, shot and wounded a cinnamon bear, this afternoon. He left his pony and crawled on his hands and knees nearly a thousand yards to get near enough for a shot; as soon as the gun was fired the bear headed for a gulley nearby. By the time Tom had remounted his pony the bear had disappeared, but he trailed the wounded animal to its lair, and a second shot ended its life. As the result of his bravery, Tom secured a necklace of bear's claws, and will henceforth have a voice in the councils of his tribe.

We find wild goose berries in abundance, but they are exceedingly sour.

Saddles are kept packed all the time now, with everything in readiness for a fight with hostiles at any moment. At night our beds consist of our saddle-blankets spread on the ground, and our saddles for pillows, and they are good ones. We lie down, shut our eyes, imagine we are covered up, and go to sleep, not to wake till morning; unless it rains, when we cover our heads with a corner of the blanket, roll over, and are soon sound asleep again.

The morning of July 10th we broke camp at five o'clock, marched 33 miles, and went into camp on the bank of Yellow Muddy Creek. This creek gets its name from the yellow mud that colours the water; and it looked to me a good deal like mush.

We have an abundance of antelope meat, and book it in different ways, the most common being to place it on coals. Of course it tastes smoky and is more or less scorched, but it is eaten with keen relish.

While riding my horse to water this evening, he took it into his head to see what he could, and having nothing on him but a halter and *lariat* I let him go it.

I was given an exhilarating ride. After running about a mile, and jumping over a ditch that was fully ten feet across and twenty-five deep, I stopped him just in time to prevent him from jumping into or over the captain's tent!

We killed a large number of rattlesnakes in the camp, and Crazy Jim skinned, cooked, and ate one, with as much relish as

I ever saw a man eat a piece of eel. He said it tasted a good deal like an eel, only it was sweeter and not so tough. There was no one in the company who wanted to borrow his frying pan after that. He stuffed the skin of the snake full of grass, and then wore it round his neck just as you would a scarf.

Crazy Jim, or James Severs, as his name really is, is from Indiana, and is a brave and ever-ready soldier. He was named Crazy Jim on the campaign last year, when, at the time of the massacre of the men on the Little Big Horn, he saved a pack mule and its load of ammunition from falling into the hands of the Indians, at the risk of his own life.

While he was after the mule the Indians fired over one hundred shots at him, but not a bullet happened to hit him, although they caused dust to fly near him in all directions. He is now wearing one stripe on his dress coat sleeve, showing that he has served one five years' enlistment, and is now on his second. He re-enlisted last winter at Fort Rice, and says he will must have a furlough this winter, as there is a girl digging leeks in Indiana that he wants to see mighty bad,

We were up very early on the morning of July 11th, and were in the saddle at 3:45. I got permission of the captain to hunt along the line of march with Private Neeley. Antelope were very thick, but a little sly. I shot my first antelope on this hunt. Neeley shot five out of one herd, and we took the hind quarters of six of them on our horses and started to join the command. They were a heavy load for our poor animals.

We got nearly nine miles from the line of march which I think is doing very well for two men in a hostile country. While we were yet about three miles from camp we saw three riders coming towards us, and we did not wait to see what they wanted but hurried on towards the camp as fast as our horses could very well travel with the heavy loads we had.

We had no extra liking for a battle on the open prairie with that kind of game, and on looking back and seeing that they were running their ponies, and seeing that we could not get to camp before they overtook us, we rode up to the foot of a bluff, and then led our horses to the top of it. We had not the least doubt but that we were in for a fight and wanted to have all the advantage on our side. We would have given all the meat we had to have been in camp at that particular time, but we did not intend to surrender; oh, no!

We waited in silence for nearly five minutes, and as the men came nearer and they did not look so much like Indians as they had but a short time before and our Indians soon proved to be three men from "E" Company, who, like ourselves, had been on a hunt, and were looking for the camp. We went down to them, and in answer to their inquiries as to what we were up there for, we said we were trying to see if we could locate the camp.

Here was a chance for one of those hair-breadth escapes so often read about, and I have no doubt but that the majority of them are about as dangerous as ours was.

There was a very hard thunder shower in the evening, and of course we men got wet, but we have got so used to being wet that it is no hardship, but it is a little disagreeable. Marched twenty miles, and camped on Red Water Creek.

CHAPTER TWENTY-SIX

Men Are Impatient

July 12th, 1877.—Broke camp this morning with rain falling, the men out of sorts and rations getting low. We do not seem to be doing anything likely to get results—merely fooling around out of reach of hostiles. It strikes me as rather queer that Colonel Otis should devote so much time to visiting abandoned Indian village sites instead of getting in actual contact with hostiles.

We are now to head back to the camp where our wagon train is parked, whence we started forth on this apparently resultless scouting expedition. We have been scouting almost six days and are so near our starting point that we can reach it in one day.

This has been a hard trip for our underfed and travel-worn horses. Today my horse lagged for the first time. I touched him with the spurs, but he did not respond; then I dismounted and led him behind the command, feeling sorry for the poor fellow. We came in sight of camp when three miles away, and my horse was more than three hours in covering the distance. Several times I thought he was going to fall down and die.

I have with this little horse kept pace with my captain all summer, and he has had two large horses at his disposal, changing mounts nearly every alternate day, so I think my mount has been an unusually good one. The captain is a great hunter and a splendid shot—I think the best in the whole regiment, either with rifle or revolver. When out hunting, in addition to my load, my horse has carried an infantry rifle with ammunition, for the captain's use, and I have followed him on many a wild chase in pursuit of game, and when he has dismounted to take a shot, I have invariably been ready to hand him his gun and hold his horse.

Marched 41 miles today.

July 13th.—Broke camp at 8 o'clock in the morning and took our own trail back towards Tongue River. No danger of finding hostiles on this trail! Went sixteen miles and camped on Cherry Creek, in a poor location. However, the ground is too rough to drill on.

I rode my lieutenant's extra horse today, as mine was only able to carry itself. The men said I looked like a mosquito on a haystack, and I guess they were right, as it is the tallest and most rangy horse with the command. I need a step-ladder to mount him with. He is docile, willing, and an easy rider.

The captain saw a bear near a ravine, about one mile from the trail, and calling me to follow, started for the game. I gave the big horse the rein and a touch of the spurs, and away we went. The bear saw us coming and turned and ran, and a bear can run! We fired at the bear with our revolvers but did not hit it, so it did not stop to give battle, but soon was out of sight in the ravine. I was surprised that the big horse made such speed. We had not been back in line long, when Colonel Otis rode alongside and asked the captain if he knew if Lieutenant Mathey wanted to sell that horse. Evidently the colonel was looking for a horse that could run!

July 14.—Were in the saddle at 7 a.m. I rode the captain's Indian pony Pete, the most contrary piece of pony I ever came in contact with. Could not get the pony started when, the command pulled out but after giving the balky beast the usual medicine and getting its nose in the right direction, I took after the troops, and the pony made good time.

Marched 25 miles and camped where there was excellent grass and good water for the horses. We remained here a number of days, then marched back to our former camping place on Sunday Creek, where a few days were given to drilling. At 4 o'clock in the afternoon we received orders to report at Tongue River, and an hour later were on the way.

At about 8 o'clock, while the troops were moving along silently and quietly, a rifle shot rang out. All was excitement, and officers rode hurriedly along, to discover who had fired the gun. As they arrived at the back end of the line, they discovered the packers crowded around someone lying on the ground, and were told that the chief packer had been shot in the head and was unconscious, evidently dying.

His comrades said the chief packer and one of his men had some words about the way the packing was done and had called each other hard names. Finally the man who did the shooting, swore that he would take the position of chief packer when the pack mules arrived at Tongue River, as he knew more about packing than any other man with the outfit, then suddenly wheeled his horse about, shot the chief packer and rode off in the darkness. The chum of the dying man a moment later, gun in hand, mounted a pony and started in pursuit of the assassin.

The murdered man left a wife and three children in one of the larger cities of Florida, where he owned considerable property. Love of adventure, and a desire to investigate the mining and agricultural inducements of the north-west, had prompted the adventure that culminated in this dire tragedy.

The body was rolled in a blanket and placed in a shallow grave by the side of the trail.

The affair was reported to General Miles, who sent a detail with an ambulance for the body, which was examined by the surgeons, enclosed in a coffin, and buried in the Military Cemetery at Tongue River.

Chapter Twenty-Seven

Once More on the Yellowstone

We reached the bank of the Yellowstone river at about midnight, and it being too dark to pitch our tents, we were ordered to unsaddle and rest as best we could until morning. So off came the saddles and down on the ground went the whole command, glad to get a chance for a little rest.

Reveille was sounded bright and early in the morning, and after a hasty breakfast we mount and march one mile, when we camp on Tongue River, nearly opposite and about one mile from the head-quarters of General Miles.

We can now look down on the *Tongue-River-ites*, and are glad once more to be where we can see some indications of civilization.

The location of the cantonment at Tongue River was the selection of General Miles, and does credit to his knowledge and foresight.

There are about 500 Cheyenne Indians camped near the post. They are under the personal supervision of General Miles. I am told that it was only through his personal exertions that the warriors of these Indians were prevented from taking the war-path, some time ago, when the man in charge of the Agency failed to pay the annuity due them from the Government. The chiefs complained to General Miles that the man in charge of the Agency at the time was "Heap cheat" Miles appealed in their behalf direct to the Government at Washington, and was told the appropriation for these Indians had been exhausted. He supplied their needs from his own scanty stores, and told them he would see that they did not suffer.

The command remained in this camp several days and then General Sturges was ordered to take six companies of the Seventh Cavalry and head Chief Joseph off from his attempt to escape into the great wilderness north of the nation's boundary line.

The hardships of our Indian campaign now began in earnest. We made forced marches and got in ahead of Chief Joseph and his warriors and tribe's people generally, at the foot of the Little Rocky Mountains, in Montana Territory, Sept. 8th, 1877. Here General Sturges halted his command, and it seemed that he wanted the Indians to take the offensive.

The reds advanced and a slight skirmish ensued, and instead of leading a charge, Sturges posted himself on a bluff, with a body guard, fully a mile from the reds, and viewed proceedings through his field glass. A bullet from a long-range gun in the hands of an Indian who knew how to shoot, struck the ground a short distance in front of the general, who lowered his glass, remarking that it was getting dangerous up there, and got out of danger.

At this time Lieutenant Hare went personally to Major Merrill, and asked permission to lead his company in a charge against the hostiles; but, of course, the request was refused. Prompt action was what the men of the Old Seventh wanted. They all felt that if "turned loose," they could and would clean out Chief Joseph and his warriors in short order.

Our loss in the long distance skirmish, which lasted but a few minutes, was three men slightly wounded; the enemy loss was about the same. Their long-range rifles are much more effective than our short-range carbines, unless we get in close quarters.

The number of warriors with Joseph, and also the non-combatants, are much less than he had when he started on his projected break for the Canadian wilds. The patrol work of United States troops is bewildering to the militant Indian chiefs, and the young bucks are not leaving reservations for the "war-path" in any considerable numbers. The reds under Sitting Bull and Crazy Horse have found "scalp hunting" poor business, and are dwindling.

But why prolong the unequal contest!

After Chief Joseph had passed through the Gap in the Mountains, General Sturges marched our force around a range of the mountains, and then, permitting the retreating Indians to again get away, followed after them. We camped several nights where they had camped the night before. At each camping place the reds had erected breastworks, prepared to give us battle.

If this is a war of attrition, they were getting the food and we were getting appetites. Rations ran short, until we had nothing to eat but buffalo meat and bull-cherries. Finally we got where we could get neither buffalo meat nor bull-cherries. Then we butchered Indian ponies. This meat was good.

General Sturges issued a bombastic card of thanks and as the document was being read by the adjutant you could hear men say, "We do not want wind pudding; give us something solid!" General Sturges sent to General Howard for rations and Howard sent us ammunition. A day later a wagon train arrived from Fort Peck, with rations. Instead of hard bread they brought flour, and salt pork that was spoiled. Each man was issued a quart of flour and a chunk of pork. We made flap-jacks. Taking a tin cup and partly filling it with wheat flour, we would add water and make a paste, and then add a piece of pork, and cook the mess. It was difficult to dig it out of the cup. It was worse than hard-tack and ancient bacon.

Sturges with six companies, every soldier fighting mad, loitered along. But when Miles was given the "right of way," he pressed after the fugitive reds, headed them off and forced Chief Joseph to surrender, after a hard fighting that lasted three days.

I was mighty glad to be "on the job" at the Battle of Snake River, and so were my comrades of Company M, Seventh Cavalry.

Some time before this event, while with Sturges, I was ordered to take a despatch to General Miles, and was to go alone over unknown land, liable at any moment to meet hostiles. I could not refuse to make the venture. Better lose my scalp than to get the name of being a coward.

Receiving the necessary instructions as to route and provided with a compass, at dusk I set forth on the hazardous ride. To say that I was startled at every little sound, would be putting it very mild. But I kept on and arrived at my destination about noon the next day. Never did a camp look so good to me as that one did. And never again do I want to take such a trip. It was over bluffs, along ravines, across stretches of prairie, expecting to get a bullet from the gun of a lurking hostile at any moment. It is no wonder that at the age of twenty-four my hair is streaked with gray.

CHAPTER TWENTY-EIGHT

Battle Between Nez Perces and Troops

The general interest in the battle between Nez Perces warriors led by Chief Joseph, and the cavalry force with General Miles in command, and the surrender of the hostiles, demands more attention than ever has appeared in print. It was the *finale* of an important campaign; it threw wide open the door that had blocked the way for the settlement of the Great North-West; it stopped trespassing on the soil of a friendly nation by disgruntled natives of this country—our wards, not wanted there, whose best interests demanded that they should cease savagery and live in peace with their white neighbours.

When Chief Joseph started forth on this final and fateful campaign, he was in command of a large force of superior and well equipped Indian warriors. With these hostiles, it was a most sacred war. From the time they left their homes in Oregon until they were attacked by the command of General Miles on Snake Creek, they had travelled sixteen hundred miles and at a rate that would have killed a cavalry horse.

This was a wonderful trip. Chief Joseph did not make it with warriors alone. He had with him all the squaws, children and aged males of the tribe, their *tepees* and other belongings. Joseph's movements were retarded, and at times diverted, by strong bodies of United States troops. He was able and shrewd, and was keen in leading pursuing columns along trails where their men and horses would suffer most for want of food and water.

Chief Joseph's warriors had dwindled to about three hundred; every one of them hardened by the difficulties of the march, able to go days without food or water, and each brave carrying a gun made for use in hunting large game. They also had a number of long range needle-guns, two of them being supplied with the most approved telescope sights. One of the rifles was a heavy Creedmore, such as is used by the most skilful shots in America on the celebrated ranges. No doubt it was one of these rifles that sent that bullet in the direction of General Sturges, during the brief skirmish at the Gap in the Mountains, which caused him to lower his field-glass and step out of range.

The failure of General Howard to land Chief Joseph, is said to be due to the fact that Howard started on the chase with his command not half supplied with equipment necessary for such a drive. As a result, Howard's movements were hampered and his fighting strength greatly reduced at the time when his force should have been at its very best.

General Howard was not versed in Indian warfare. He found there is a vast difference between Agency-life and its treaty making and fighting Indians. It was Howard's lack of tact that impelled Joseph and his brother White Bird and the rest of the Nez Perces to reject the demand of Howard. They did not want to fight; they wanted to escape to a land of refuge, where they could live in peace. This is the Indians' side of the story.

Chief Joseph continued on his retreat through the northern mountains. On August 9th General Gibbons came into ineffectual contact with him at the Big Hole Mountains.

When General Miles started from the mouth of Tongue River, September 18th, to attack Chief Joseph, he had formed his plans so well that victory was assured. He struck Chief Joseph's camp the 30th of September, 1877, after marching twelve days, at the very place he said he would before setting out from Tongue River. The men under Miles were eager for the fray. As soon as the Indians were seen General Miles, without hesitation, placed himself in front of the troops, and at once the first order was given. It was:—

"Charge!!"

The battle was on!

Ahead went our three companies of the Seventh Cavalry, direct for the Indians, each man trying to be the first to draw blood.

Never was a more gallant charge made by any troops.

The Second Cavalry had been ordered to round up and look after the ponies of the reds, and this placed the burden of the fight on the three companies of the Seventh Cavalry. The charges on the reds and on their ponies were simultaneous.

Two men reel in their saddles and fall to the ground at the beginning of the charge. There is no faltering, spurs hasten to the utmost the speed of the horses. We soon come to where the ground is so cut up by natural rifle-pits that our horses can advance no further. The Indians are firing rapidly; our men are responding.

Halt!—is the shrill bugle command.

Then *Dismount!*—and *Prepare to Fight on Foot!*

And this is what was done, and with as much coolness as though we were on parade, instead of being where bullets are whistling.

As soon as our men dismount the carbines begin to talk to the Indians so fast and with such good results, that the fire of the reds slackens, as they take to cover, but soon they are firing more rapidly than before.

General Miles gave orders for the men to shelter themselves as much as they could and to make their shots count. Men got behind anything that would afford the least shelter, and some dug into the earth with entrenching tools. We lay there and shot at every moving thing seen above the tops of the breastworks of the reds. There are many men in the command who never before were under fire, and they are as aggressive and cool as the veterans.

A man falls on the right of the line—or, rather, rises and then falls! He was lying down when a rifle bullet hit him in the shoulder. He springs to his feet in agony, and instantly falls, and rolls behind a little pile of dirt, and tries to grasp his carbine, but he cannot do so with hands benumbed, and sinks back as though dead!

There he lies until darkness makes it safe for comrades to go to his relief. He was found alive, and taken to the hospital tent on a stretcher, where the surgeon dressed the wound and he soon became conscious. It is Private Deitline, of Company M. The surgeon says he is badly wounded, but will pull through all right. Good, for we all like him; he is our company farrier.

Other wounded men are taken to the hospital. We soon get over the nausea at first caused by the sight of wounds and blood, and assist in caring for the injured.

The first sergeant of Company M is found dead, shot through the lungs, while in the front row of little ditches our men had dug in order to press closer to the entrenched Indians; he is the man who declared when bidding his wife and children goodbye, as our force left Fort Rice last spring, that he had a presentment that they would not see him again.

The body was placed in a grave, over which a volley was fired.

During the battle, Lieutenant Eckerson with a few men distinguished themselves, when horses attached to the mountain howitzer were shot while the piece was being hauled into position. The lieutenant leaped from his horse, cut the traces, helped the men place the gun in position, and fired shot after shot.

Trumpeter Herwood saved the life of his captain and thereby came near sacrificing his own. He saw an Indian taking careful aim at the captain, and deliberately stepped in front of his officer receiving the bullet in his own side. When bringing in the wounded we found Harwood lying on the ridge where he had fallen, and told Surgeon Havre that the man was so badly wounded that we feared he would bleed to death while being carried to the hospital. The surgeon made examination and said: "He can't live; take in those who have a chance to recover."

The next morning, while being attended to at the hospital

tent by Surgeon Havre, Trumpeter Herwood said: "I am the man you left on the ridge to die! If you are going to probe my wound with a finger, as you did last night, please cut the nail off!"

We dug rifle pits, both day and night and got nearer and nearer the enemy. Chief Joseph's entire camp was surrounded the first day of the fight, but that was not enough to make him yield. He had sufficient food and ammunition for a siege.

On ascertaining this fact, after Chief Joseph had refused to surrender, General Miles had a series of rifle pits dug that cut off the water supply of the reds. Chief Joseph was not slow to discover this fact, and seeing that he could not possibly escape from the trap he was in, or defeat the white force, he held a council at which it was decided to surrender to General Miles! This emphasized their dislike for General Howard, the department commander, to whom they attributed the troubles that had started them afield.

CHAPTER TWENTY-NINE

White Bird Takes Flight

When the Nez Perces war chiefs decided to make the surrender to General Miles, Chief Joseph had a piece of white cloth displayed and came to our headquarters, all alone. He was received by General Miles, and in a subdued voice said his chiefs and warriors wanted to surrender.

How we did cheer when that piece of white cloth appeared! Our work was done—and well done, too!

General Howard had arrived on the scene while the battle was in progress, accompanied by an escort of seventeen men. He commended General Miles, saying in what seemed a rather bombastic manner:—

"General, I find everything all right. This is your fight, and I want to say amen to everything that you have done."

But notice the difference in tone of the report of the matter issued by General Howard, and the general order of General Miles, printed in the chapter that follows.

While Chief Joseph was on his way to meet General Miles, at the time he surrendered, he passed by General Howard without paying any attention to him, and walked deliberately up to Miles and said: "I want to surrender to you!"

As the noted Indian stood there a self-acknowledged prisoner, rifle in hand, his bearing was calm and deliberate, he was indeed a brave!

Chief Joseph is about thirty-five years of age, five feet ten inches in height. His clothing consisted of blanket-trousers, beaded leggings, beaded buckskin moccasins, and a fine blanket. His features are regular, his black eyes are as piercing as an eagle's.

His long black hair is gathered in a loose braid at the back of his head, his scalp-lock is ornamented with a cluster of feathers, and long braids hang in front of his ears.

Such is the young man, who for a long time had bid defiance to what he considered unjust and oppressive mandates on the part of the Government of the United States, and who had repulsed in turn military forces commanded by Howard, Sturges, and Gibbons, and for three days had held out against General Miles.

As he addressed General Miles, he handed the general his rifle, with the muzzle pointed towards the ground. When the weapon had thus changed hands the chief stepped to one side, saying "*How!*" as he did so. Then several other chiefs and warriors who had followed Chief Joseph, as in ceremonial order, advanced one at a time, each surrendering his rifle to General Miles.

To those privileged to witness this remarkable scene, it did not seem as if these captives were savages. Surely, they were Knights of the plains and mountains and forests. Fairly defeated, they surrendered their weapons; not lances and shields, but death-dealing rifles, the very best that American inventors were able to produce.

The ceremony of surrender, one the part of the Indians, began at 2 o'clock in the afternoon on the 5th day of October, 1877, and it continued in the same deliberate manner till the close of day. From time to time Indians left their rifle pits, singly or in small groups, and coming to the headquarters of General Miles gave themselves up as prisoners of war. Even when night set in, the entire band had not given themselves up, and our lines of sentinels were kept posted. When the sun appeared next morning the surrenders were continued.

The first day 67 warrior and their squaws and children came in, the next day the number was increased to 290 men, women and children. Then we took possession of their trenches and camp. Forty wounded Indians were discovered. They were being cared for by squaws. Only two dead Indians were located. The disposition they had made of their dead remained a mystery. We were certain that thirty or more warriors were killed outright when we made our first charge, and they lost many more during the progress of the engagement.

"White Bird" failed to appear with the other reds, and could not be located—he had flown.

Our loss was two officers and twenty-six men killed and four officers and forty-two men wounded.

I sustained an injury to my back, which seemed of little moment, and caused me practically no trouble for some time, but later developed spinal trouble of so serious a nature that one side was partly and my legs entirely paralyzed. While on scout duty with a detail, in going down a mountain, my horse stumbled, sending me headlong, and in falling the horse landed across my body. I was soon back in the saddle and continued with the detail.

The Indians having surrendered, the next thing to be done was to provide transportation and convey our sick and wounded to the Missouri river. There were only three ambulances with the command, and more than forty wounded to be carried. A number of the heavy, jolting army wagons were requisitioned, and also *travoys* made on which to carry the wounded. A *travoy* is made by fastening a long pole on each side, of a pony, with the ends on the ground, with a piece of heavy canvass swung hammock-like between the poles. It is a crude device and a source of constant torture to a patient as it is jolted along.

The journey to the Missouri River ended October 20th, when our sick and wounded were transferred by a steamboat to military hospitals at Forts Rice, Lincoln and Buford for treatment.

The captive Nez Perces were taken to Bismarck, and paraded through the main street of the city, with Chief Joseph on an Indian pony in the lead. He was "honour guest "at a banquet given that evening, and conducted himself with dignity and reserve.

These Indians were for some time kept on exhibition at Bismarck, and then were placed in cars and shipped to Fort Leavenworth, Kansas.

Sergeant McDermott, who was killed at the Battle of Snake Creek, was a gentleman. He was liked by all the men in his company, and respected by officers and men throughout the regiment.

He was honourably discharged in June, by reason of the expiration of his term of enlistment. He at once re-enlisted and took a furlough for three months to visit relatives and friends in the East. While there enjoying himself, he learned that his regiment was to take part in a strenuous campaign against the Indians. With true soldier spirit, he threw up his furlough and hastened to join his company, which he reached in July. Asked by a comrade why he did not stay his time out, Sergeant McDermott said:—

"If the boys are in for a fight, I want to be with them. When the campaign is over, I will take another furlough and go and finish my visit."

CHAPTER THIRTY

Surrender of the Nez Perces Indians

The documents that follow, form a part of the historical record of the War with the Nez Perces, and deserve the most careful perusal by all readers. They have been discussed in the public press, and for obvious reasons:

REPORT OF GENERAL HOWARD

In the Field, Steamer *Benton*,
Missouri River, Oct. 10, 1877,

General P. H. Sheridan,
Commanding Division of the Missouri:—

It is due you, as commander of this military division, to know the facts that I have already telegraphed to General McDowell from the battlefield concerning the final operations and surrender of the Nez Perces.

First, on the 11th of September I assumed command of General Sturges's troops after I had passed him at Clarke's Fork, and he operated in conjunction with my force proper till the close.

The advance, Sturges immediately commanding, then made a forced march of eighty-five miles in two days, struck the hostiles, captured quite a number of their ponies, killed and wounded several warriors and drove them beyond the Musselshell.

The 12th of September I sent from Clarke's Forks, a despatch to General Miles showing him that the Indians were making for the Musselshell country by exceedingly long marches, and urging unusual activity, and requesting him to make every effort in his power to prevent the escape of the hostile band. General Miles received the despatch at Tongue River on the evening of the 16th, and promptly moved his command—two battalions of the Second and Seventh Cavalry, and one his own mounted infantry—on the 17th, to the mouth of the Musselshell River.

Meanwhile, as he requested nine days to get into position, I slowed my march to about fifteen miles a day, knowing that the hostiles were watching me and would do the same. They slackened their pace after crossing the Missouri at Cow Island.

As soon as Miles found out that they were beyond the Missouri he crossed where he was, and made forced marches across our front to the north of Bear Paw Mountain, and struck the Indians about seven o'clock a.m. of the 30th *ult*. They were camped near a creek bottom, in a strong natural position, but their numerous ponies, (now nearly worn out), were scattered over the open country grazing.

Miles charged the camp and herd simultaneously A desperate fight occurred, in which two officers and twenty-five men were killed, and four officers and forty -two men wounded.

The ponies were nearly all captured—some seven hundred; but the Indians, hemmed in by Miles's pickets, held out until after my arrival, (firing was then going on), the evening of the fourth. I had with me two friendly Nez Perces and an interpreter. The two Nez Perces were sent the next morning into the hostile camp. Through them the surrender was arranged. A few Indians, including White Bird, crept through the lines during the night.

A portion of my artillery and infantry and Sturges's cavalry were brought up within twenty-five miles of the battlefield; but as the Sioux under Sitting Bull continued quiet, I deemed it best, on account of the difficulty of supplying the command, to return the foot troops to the Missouri.

Sturges's cavalry were ordered to report back to General Miles, and moved in conjunction with him back to the mouth of the Musselshell.

I embarked my troops on the steamer *Benton*. On account of Sitting Bull's proximity, I delayed their departure from the 10th to the 13th, until Miles, burdened with the wounded and the Indian prisoners—375 in number—had reached the Missouri.

Colonel Sturges and his regiment deserve special credit for energetic, persistent and successful work.

General Miles and his command have and deserve the great honour of the final battle and surrender, while appreciation and gratitude are due our officers and men who engaged the hostiles in Idaho, have cheerfully made forced marches for 1,600 miles, were part of the last operating force north of the Missouri, and were represented by their commander at the surrender.

I directed General Miles to keep the prisoners till next spring, it being too late to send them to Idaho by direct routes this fall and too costly by steamer or rail.

[Signed,]   O. O. Howard

Commanding Department.

———

ORDER OF GENERAL MILES

In the Field,
Camp Near Bear Paw Mountain, M. T.
October 7th, 1877.

[GENERAL ORDERS No. 3,]

The commanding officer takes great pleasure in expressing to his command his congratulations for the recent exhibition they have given of the highest degree of endurance under hardship, and unyielding fortitude in battle. The secret forced marches that enabled you to surprise the enemy when in fancied security, the resistless charge that at once shut them in the fastness of their camp, and the courageous fight, with death and maiming thick about you, are all your own.

In the entire success that has attended your efforts, the capture of Chief Joseph and his followers, the entire country will share, with gratitude to you who have accomplished so much.

It is an added source of congratulation that General O. O. Howard, who has so persistently waged war against these hostile Nez Perces and driven them from the slope of the Pacific to this remote country, was present to witness the completion of his arduous and thankless undertaking.

[Signed,]   N. A. Miles,
General in Command.

CHAPTER THIRTY-ONE

Hospital Staff Commended

While we were on the way to the Missouri River, I was at times in great distress, due to the injury to my back sustained when my horse fell on me, as heretofore noted. Our surgeon gave me a "going over" when we reached the river, and told me that I must accompany the wounded to a hospital that only rest and the best of care would prevent complete collapse. He booked me for a steamboat ride down the Missouri along with my sick and wounded comrades.

After a long and tedious ride on board the steamboat, we arrive at Fort Rice, and the injured who could do so walked to the army hospital, the others being carried on stretchers. We were not a nice looking lot. We were soon arranged in the ward and once more greet Surgeon Taylor, who visits each man, washes and dresses wounds, sees that proper medicines are provided, and those that cannot wash themselves are bathed and that all are provided with clean under garments. He is ably assisted by Steward Von Clausen and three nurses from the infantry.

Assistant Steward Gallenne, who was shot in his left ankle during our last fight with the Indians, had the leg amputed. He had a cot next to mine. We agreed that if Sturges and Howard had pushed on instead of taking it easy, they could have whipped Chief Joseph before he struck the fork, and that if they had done so Gallenne would now be a leg ahead and that my back and legs would not have been rendered useless.

We sat on our cots and talked over our army experiences,

and acclaimed General Custer and General Miles as our ideals of what commanders sent out to end an Indian uprising should be.

As the days passed, and hospital patients began to recover, we resorted to various sources of amusement. Trumpeter Harwood, or Doctor Scroggs, was a tremendous success—he was a combined circus and menagerie. He is the man shot through the shoulder, who was left on the battlefield to die after the surgeon said he could not live to be taken to the hospital, at our battle with Chief Joseph. There was not a place in the hospital that he did not visit. He would go around, feeling the pulses of different men, get off comical remarks in explaining the disease or wound; to one he would prescribe a quart or more of whiskey, to another a promotion, to another a sutlership, to another a perpetual furlough under full pay, etc. He would get men to laughing whom he found despondent.

Dr. Scroggs was as solemn as the proverbial deacon when Surgeon Taylor was in the ward.

Then there was McCurren, who was shot in the hand and had also lost a finger, and always told the surgeon that the hand was so stiff and sore he could not use it, yet as soon as the surgeon had crossed the parade to his quarters, he would grab a broom and go through the manual of arms without flinching. He was stiff and sore for a discharge, and he got it, too!

Blacksmith Deitline was shot in the right shoulder—he is the man who sprang to his feet at the time he was shot and he was severely wounded in the head afterwards by a chance bullet as he lay on the ground. He would tell the surgeon how he felt, and say he was not able to raise his arm, and asking the surgeon if he thought its use would ever be restored, he would work the arm as much as he could, the while wincing with pain. He was not working for a discharge; he wanted to recover from the injury.

There were others in the ward that were lively and cheerful, and we did have fun at times. But it was not fun to see the serious wounds dressed, and to hear the men groan as a piece of bone was removed or a bad spot was burned out with caustic.

There was a soldier in the ward who had lost his reason, due a wound in the head. He almost constantly talked about Indians, and after he had tried to insert the tines of a table-fork in an ear to dig the Indians out, he was placed in a straight jacket. The day before that was done, fearing that the galvanic battery would be used on him, he sneaked into the dispensary and destroyed the machine. I had reason to be sorry for that, as the galvanic battery was being used daily in the treatment I received, and it was the only one available.

The hardest feature of military life is to be a patient in a military hospital.

On the 1st of December eight of us were able to get about on crutches and were permitted to take exercise out of doors. We would line up and race for the sutler's store, the last man in to pay for the cigars

Taken as a whole, the diet and the regular meals at Fort Rice hospital were excellent and abundant. Even fresh eggs were provided. Surgeon Taylor each day inspected the kitchen and would taste and smell of food prepared for the men, rejecting any food that was not just what it should be.

Chapter Thirty-Two

Report of General Custer

As convalescence progressed, the men spent considerable time in discussing the Indian campaigns in which they had taken part, the different methods of warfare with the reds, and their likes and dislikes of commanding officers. Disapproval of commanders who had failed to get results was unanimous, and the men praised Custer and Miles to the limit. General Custer had a "way of his own" as an Indian fighter, and for a number of years had kept the hostiles busy in the very section in which we had been campaigning, and when Sitting Bull was "on the rampage," we present an official report he made while in the field. It is illuminating and instructive:

Official Report of General Custer
[Copy.]
Headquarters Battalion Seventh Cavalry,
Pompey's Pillar, Yellowstone River, Montana,
August 15th, 1873.
Acting Assistant Adjutant-General Yellowstone
   Expedition:
Sir,—Acting under the instructions of the Brevet-Major-General commanding, I proceeded at five o'clock, on the morning of the 4th instant, with one squadron of my command, numbering about ninety men, to explore a route over which the main column could move. Having reached a point on the Yellowstone River, near the mouth of Tongue River, and several miles in advance, and

while waiting the arrival of the forces of the expedition, six mounted Sioux dashed boldly into the skirt of the timber within which my command had halted and unsaddled, and attempted to stampede our horses. Fortunately the *vedettes* discovered the approach of the Indians in time to give the alarm.

A few well-directed shots soon drove the Indians to a safe distance, where they kept up a series of yells, occasionally firing a few shots. As soon as the squadron could mount, I directed Captain Moylan to move out in pursuit, at the same time I moved with the troops in advance, commanded by First Lieutenant T. W. Custer.

Following the Indians at a brisk gait, my suspicions became excited by the confident bearing exhibited by the six Sioux in our front, whose course seemed to lead us near a heavy growth of timber which stood along the river bank above us. When almost within rifle range of this timber, I directed the squadron to halt, while I with two orderlies, all being well mounted, continued after the Sioux in order to develop their intentions.

Proceeding a few hundred yards in advance of the squadron, and keeping a watchful eye on the timber to my left, I halted. The six Indians in my front also halted, as if to tempt further pursuit. Finding all efforts in this direction unavailing, their plans and intentions were quickly made evident, as no sooner was it seen that we intended to advance no farther, than with their characteristic howls and yells over three hundred well-mounted warriors dashed in perfect line from the edge of the timber, and charged down upon Captain Moylan's squadron, at the same time endeavouring to intercept the small party with me.

As soon as the speed of the thoroughbred on which I was mounted brought me within hailing distance of Lieutenant Custer's troop, I directed that officer to quickly throw forward a dismounted line of troopers, and endeavour to empty a few Indian saddles. The order was obeyed with the greatest alacrity, and as the Sioux came dashing forward, expecting to ride down the squadron, a line of dismounted cavalrymen rose from the grass and delivered almost in the faces of the warriors a volley of carbine bullets which broke and scattered their ranks in all directions, and sent more than one Sioux reeling from the saddle.

This check gave us time to make our dispositions to resist the succeeding attacks, which we knew our enemies would soon make upon us. The great superiority of our enemies in numbers, the long distance separating us from the main command, and the belief, afterwards verified, that the woods above us still concealed a portion of the savage forces, induced me to confine my movements, at first, strictly to the defensive.

The entire squadron (except the horse-holders) was dismounted and ordered to fight on foot. The Indians outnumbering us almost five to one, were enabled to envelope us completely between their lines formed in a semicircle, and the river which flowed at our backs. The little belt of timber in which we had been first attacked formed a very good cover for our led-horses, while the crest of a second table-land, conveniently located from the timber, gave us an excellent line of defence.

The length of our line and the numbers of the enemy prevented us from having any force in reserve; every available officer and man was on the skirmish-line, which was really our line of battle, even the number of men holding horses had to be reduced, so that each horse-holder held eight horses. Until the Indians were made to taste quite freely of our lead they displayed unusual boldness, frequently charging up to our line and firing with great deliberation and accuracy.

Captain Moylan exercised command along the entire line; Lieutenant Custer commanded the centre; my adjutant, Lieutenant James Calhoun commander the right; and Lieutenant Charles A. Varnum, the left. The first Indian killed was shot from his pony by "Bloody Knife," the Crow who acted as my guide and scout. Soon after, Private Charles P. Miller, of A troop, Seventh Cavalry, succeeded in sending a carbine bullet directly through the body of a chief who had been conspicuous throughout the engagement.

At the same time it was known that our firing had disabled many of their ponies, while owing to our sheltered position the only damage thus far inflicted upon us was one man and two horses wounded, one of the latter shot in three places.

Finding their efforts to force back our line unavailing, the Indians now resorted to another expedient. By an evidently preconcerted plan they set fire in several places, to the tall grass which covered the ground in our front hoping by this means to force us back to the rear, and thus finish us at their pleasure.

Fortunately for us there was no wind prevailing at the time, while the grass was scarcely dry enough to burn rapidly. Taking advantage of the dense curtain of smoke which rose from the burning grass, the Indians, by following the course of the flames, could often contrive to obtain a shot at us at a comparatively close range; but my men, observing that there was no danger to be apprehended from the slowly advancing flames, could frequently catch an opportunity to send a shot through a break in the curtain of smoke, and in this way surprised the Indian by the adoption of his own device.

The fight began at 11:30 a. m., and was waged without cessation until three o'clock, all efforts of the Indians to dislodge us proving unsuccessful. The Indians had become extremely weary, and had almost discontinued their offensive movements, when my ammunition ran low. I decided to mount the squadron and charge the Indians, with the intention of driving them from the field.

Captain Moylan promptly had his men in the saddle, and

throwing twenty mounted skirmishers, under Lieutenant Varnum, the entire squadron moved forward at a trot. No sooner did the Indians discern our intentions than, despite their superiority in numbers, they cowardly prepared for flight, in which preparation they were greatly hastened when Captain Moylan's squadron charged them and drove them "pell-mell" for three miles.

Five ponies killed or badly wounded were left on the battle ground or along the line of their flight. So rapidly were they forced to flee that they abandoned and threw away breech-loading arms, saddle equipments, clothing, robes, *lariats*, and other articles comprised in an Indian outfit.

Among the Indians who fought us on this occasion were some of the identical warriors who committed the massacre at Fort Phil. Kearney, and they no doubt intended a similar program when they sent the six warriors to dash up and attempt to decoy us into a pursuit past the timber in which the savages hoped to ambush us. Had we pursued the six warriors half a mile farther, instead of halting, the entire band would have been in our rear.

So far as the troops attacked were concerned, the Indians, to offset their own heavy losses, had been able to do us no damage except to wound one man and two horses; but unfortunately two non-combatants, Veterinary Surgeon John Hosinger, Seventh Cavalry, and Mr. Baliran, of Memphis, Tenn., in endeavouring to come from the main column to join the squadron in advance, were discovered by the Indians during the attack, and being unarmed were overtaken and killed almost within view of the battleground. Fortunately the Indians were so pressed as not to be able to scalp or otherwise mutilate the remains.

On the 8th instant we discovered the trail of a large village, evidently to which the party that had attacked us on the 4th belonged. The course of the trail led up the Yellowstone, and apparently was not more than two days old. Acting under the authority of the brevet-major-general commanding, I ordered my command, consisting of four squadrons of the Seventh Cavalry, in readiness to begin the pursuit that night.

The brevet-major-general also directed the detachment of guides and Indian scouts under Lieutenant Daniel H. Brush, 17th Infantry, to report to me for temporary service. Leaving all tents and wagons behind: and taking with us rations for seven days, we started in pursuit at 10 o'clock on the night of the 8th instant, having waited until that hour until the moon should enable us to follow the trail.

Following the trail as rapidly as the rough character of the country would permit, daylight next morning found us nearly thirty miles from our starting-point. Concealing horses and men in a ravine a halt of three hours was ordered to enable the horses to graze and the men to obtain refreshments. Renewing the march at eight o'clock, the pursuit was continued without halting until noon, when, to avoid discovery, as well as to obtain needed rest for men and animals, it was decided to conceal ourselves in the timber, and await the cover of night to continue the pursuit.

Starting out at 6:30 p. m., the trail was followed rapidly for six miles, when, to our disappointment, we discovered that the Indians had taken to the river, and crossed to the east side. In following their trail to this point it was evident that the movement of the Indians was one of precipitate flight, the result of the engagement on the 4th. All along their trail and in their camping-places were to be found large quantities of what constituted Indian equipments, such as lodge-poles, robes, saddle equipments, arms, and cooking utensils In a hastily abandoned camp-ground nearly two hundred axes, besides a great many camp-kettles and cups, were found.

My entire command was disappointed when the trail showed that the Indians had crossed to the other side, particularly as our rapid marching had carried us to the point of crossing, the evening of the day on which the last of the Indians had crossed over, so that one more march would have enabled us to overhaul them. Bivouacking in a belt of timber on the river bank, we waited until daylight to begin to attempt to cross the command over the river, which at this point is about six hundred yards wide.

At early dawn the entire command forded the river to an island located in the middle of the channel; but our difficulties in the way of crossing here began, as the volume of water and the entire force of the current were to be encountered between the island and the opposite bank— the current here rushes by with a velocity of about seven miles an hour, while the depth of the water was such that a horse attempting to cross would be forced to swim several hundred yards.

Still as we knew the Indians had not discovered our pursuit, and were probably located within easy striking distance of the river, it was most desirable that a crossing should be effected. To accomplish this, Lieutenant Weston, Seventh Cavalry, with three accomplished swimmers from the command, attempted to cross on a log-raft, carrying a cable made of *lariats*. The current was so strong that Lieutenant Weston's party were unable to effect a landing, but were swept down the river nearly two miles, and then forced to abandon the raft and swim to shore.

Lieutenant Weston, with characteristic perseverance and energy, made repeated attempts afterwards to carry the cable over, but although succeeding in reaching the opposite bank in person, was unable to connect the cable with the shore.

Almost the entire day was spent in these unsuccessful efforts, until finally a crossing in this manner had to be abandoned. I then caused some cattle to be killed, and by stretching the hides over a kind of basket-frame prepared by the Crow guide, made what are known among the Indians as bull-boats; with these I hoped to be able to connect the cable with the opposite bank at daylight next morning, but just at sunset a small party of Indians were seen to ride down to the bank opposite us and water their ponies. They discovered our presence, and at once hastened away. Of course it was useless now to attempt a surprise, and the intention to cross the river the following morning was abandoned.

At early dawn the next day (the 11th instant), the Indians appeared in strong force on the river bank opposite us, and opened a brisk fire upon us from their rifles. No attention was paid to them until encouraged by this they had collected at several points in full view, and within range of our rifles, when about thirty of our best marksmen, having posted themselves along the bank, opened a well-directed fire upon the Indians and drove them back to cover.

In the meantime strong parties of Indians were reported by our pickets to be crossing the river below us, their ponies and themselves being so accustomed to the river as to render this operation quite practicable to them. Captain French, commanding the right wing, was directed to watch the parties crossing below, while Colonel Hart, commanding the right wing, posted a force to discharge this duty with regard to parties crossing above.

It would have been possible, perhaps, for us to have prevented the Indians from making a crossing, at least when they did, but I was not only willing but anxious that as many of them should come over as were so disposed. They were soon reported as moving to the bluffs immediately in rear of us from the river. Lieutenant Brush was directed to employ his scouts in watching and reporting their movements—a duty which they discharged in a thorough manner.

While this was transpiring I had mounted my command and formed it in line close under the bluffs facing from the river, where we quietly waited the attack of the Indians in our front. The sharp-shooting across the river still continued, the Indians having collected some of their best shots—apparently armed with long-range rifles—and were attempting to drive our men back from the water's edge. It was at this time that my standing orderly, Private Tuttle, of E troop, Seventh Cavalry, one of the best marksmen in my command, took a sporting Springfield rifle and posted himself, with two other men, behind cover on the river bank, and began picking off the Indians as they exposed themselves on the opposite bank.

He had obtained the range of the enemy's position early in the morning, and was able to place his shots wherever desired. It was while so engaged that he observed an Indian in full view near the river. Calling the attention of his comrade to the fact, he asked him "to watch me drop that Indian," a feat which he succeeded in performing.

Several other Indians rushed to the assistance of their fallen comrade, when Private Tuttle, by a skilful and rapid use of his breech-loading Springfield, succeeded in killing two other warriors. The Indians, enraged no doubt at this rough handling, directed their aim at Private Tuttle, who fell pierced through the head by a rifle bullet He was one of the most useful and daring soldiers who ever served under my command.

About this time Captain French, who was engaged with the Indians who were attacking us from below, succeeded in shooting a warrior from his saddle, while several ponies were known to be wounded or disabled. The Indians now began to display a strong force in our front on the bluffs. Colonel Hart was ordered to push a line of dismounted men to the crest, and prevent the further advance of the enemy towards the river.

This duty was handsomely performed by a portion of Captain Yates's squadron. Colonel Hart had posted Lieutenant Charles Braden and twenty men on a small knoll which commanded our left. Against this party the Indians made their first onslaught. A mounted party of warriors, numbering nearly two hundred, rode boldly to within thirty yards of Lieutenant Braden's position, when the latter and his command delivered such a well-directed fire that the Indians were driven rapidly from that part of the field, after having evidently suffered considerable loss.

Unfortunately Lieutenant Braden received a rifle-ball through the upper part of the thigh, passing directly through the bone, but he maintained his position with gallantry and coolness until he had repulsed the enemy. Hundreds of Indians were now to be seen galloping up and down along our front, each moment becoming bolder owing to the smallness of our force which was then visible.

Believing the proper time had arrived to assume the offensive, orders to this effect were accordingly sent to Colonel Hart and Captain French, the two wing commanders. Lieutenant Weston was directed to move his troop, L, up a deep ravine to our left, which would convey him to the enemy's position, and as soon as an opportunity occurred he was to charge them, and pursue the Indians with all the vigour practicable. Immediately after, Captain Owen Hale was directed to move his squadron, consisting of E and K troops, in conjunction with L troop, and the three to charge simultaneously. Similar dispositions were ordered in the centre and right. Lieutenant Custer, commanding B troop, was ordered to advance and charge the Indians in front of our centre, while Captains Yates and Moylan moved rapidly forward in the same direction.

Before this movement began, it became necessary to dislodge a large party of Indians posted in a ravine behind rocks in our front, who were engaged in keeping up a heavy fire upon our troops while the latter were forming. It was at this point that the horse of Lieutenant Hiram H. Ketchum, acting-assistant-adjutant-general of the expedition, was shot under him. My own horse was also shot under me within a few paces of the latter.

The duty of driving the Indians engaged in sharp-shooting entrusted to Lieutenant Charles A. Varnum, Seventh Cavalry, with a detachment of A troop of the Seventh Cavalry, soon forced the Indians back from their cover.

Everything being in readiness for a general advance, the charge was ordered and the squadrons took the gallop to the tune of "Garryowen," the band being posted immediately in rear of the skirmish line. The Indians had evidently come out prepared to do their best, and with no misgivings as to their success, as the mounds and high bluffs beyond the river were covered with groups of old men, squaws, and children, who had collected there to witness our destruction.

In this instance the proverbial power of music to soothe the savage breast utterly failed for no sooner did the band strike up the cheery notes of "Garryowen," and the squadrons advance to the charge, than the Indians exhibited unmistakable signs of commotion, and their resistance became more feeble, until finally satisfied of the earnestness of our attack they turned their ponies' heads and began a disorderly flight. The cavalry put spurs to their horses and dashed forward in pursuit, the various troop and squadron commanders vying with one another as to who should head the advance.

The appearance of the main command in sight, down the valley, at this moment, enabled me to relieve Captain French's command below us, and he was ordered to join in the pursuit. Lieutenant McIntosh, commanding G troop, moved his command up the valley at a gallop, and prevented many of the Indians from crossing. The chase was continued with the utmost vigour until the Indians were completely dispersed, and driven a distance of nine miles from where the engagement took place, and they were here forced back across the Yellowstone, the last pony killed in the attack being shot fully eight miles from the point of attack.

The number of Indians opposed to us has been estimated by the various officers engaged as from eight hundred to a thousand. My command numbered four hundred and fifty, including officers and men. The Indians were made up of different bands of Sioux, principally Uncpapas, the whole under command of "Sitting Bull," who participated in the second day's fight, and who for once has been taught a lesson he will not soon forget.

A large number of Indians who fought us were fresh from their reservations on the Missouri river. Many of the warriors engaged in the fight on both days were dressed in complete suits of the clothes issued at the agencies to the Indians. The arms with which they fought us (several of which we captured in the fight) were of the latest improved patterns of breech loading repeating rifles, and their supply of metallic rifle-cartridges seemed unlimited, as they were anything but sparing in their use.

So amply were they supplied with breech-loading rifles and ammunition that neither bows nor arrows were employed against us. As an evidence that these Indians, at least many of them, were recently from the Missouri river agencies, we found provisions, such as coffee, in their abandoned camps, and cooking and other domestic utensils, such as only reservation Indians are supplied with. Besides, our scouts conversed with them across the river for nearly an hour before the fight became general, and satisfied themselves as to the identity of their foes.

I only regret that it was impossible for my command to effect a crossing of the river before our presence was discovered, and while the hostile village was located near at hand, as I am confident that we could have largely reduced the necessity for appropriating for Indian supplies for the coming winter.

The losses of the Indians in ponies were particularly heavy, while we know their losses in killed and wounded were beyond all proportion to that which they were enabled to

inflict upon us, our losses being one officer badly wounded, four men killed, and three wounded; four horses killed
and four wounded.

Careful investigation justifies the statement that including
both days' battles, the Indians' losses will number forty
warriors, while their wounded on the opposite bank of
the river may increase this number.

Respectfully submitted.

    [Signed,]   G. A. Custer,

                              Lieutenant-Colonel 7th Cavalry,

                Brevet-Major-General, U. S. A., Commanding.

CHAPTER THIRTY-THREE

Skeletons Strewn Over Scene of Battle

About fourteen months after "Custer's Last Charge," on the Little Big Horn, while our force was on Tongue River, I was included in a detail ordered on a scout into the Big Horn country, and also to act as escort of a few officers who wished to see the battlefield where Custer and his men met death.

Some say that the distance from Tongue River, near the mountains, to the battlefield, does not exceed twenty-five miles; others place the estimate at thirty and none over thirty-five—but we, after two long and hard days' ride from the head of the Little Horn in the mountains, a point nearer than Tongue River, at present General Miles's headquarters, carefully compute the distance to be at least forty-five miles.

Beginning with the noble table-land upon which we stood, the ground gradually and gently fell towards the river, straightening out as level as a floor, and with both sides clearly defined by the sparsely shaded streams and the bluffs.

Beyond the water appeared the rugged embankment, extending from the south (where Reno held his force while Custer and his command were struggling in *the jaws of death*,) to the limit of vision on the north, standing perpendicular, save an occasional gap through which some trickling stream contributed its mite to the general volume of the Little Horn, or through which entrance to the fords are made, and through which we must ride if we would gain the other side.

Still farther back, towards the Rosebud, the silent timberless, sandy Wolf Mountains loomed high, casting a mild and pleasing shadow over the landscape, while at the other extremity of the valley the gradual divides, rich with verdure and bright-hued with full blown flowers, completed as beautiful a scene as the eye of an artist ever rested on, or the hand of a master ever transferred to canvas.

At last, after a weary march, and not without the many little incidents which go to liven up, and sometimes to still further depress the drooping spirits of man and beast, we arrived at and entered the site of the old Indian village, hard by which General Custer and his men were trapped and slaughtered.

This camping place was about four miles long, a half-mile wide, and located by the river side, upon a depressed table-land with a thin growth of timber, which at one time extended all over the bottom, but the felling of the trees by the squaws to secure the bark for food for ponies during the winters, had left the central portion of the strip almost barren.

At the southern side, we passed through a dense, bushy grove, covering three or four acres, where the squaws and papooses were concealed when Custer approached, and until the Cavalry were securely trapped.

Beyond this the ground presented a strange spectacle. *Tepee* and lodge poles were as thick as they could stand, while all about camp equipage and hides were scattered in confusion.

An outstanding feature was the great quantities of leggings lying about, and the only explanation is, that the Indians discarded them for articles of clothing taken from the dead soldiers.

Farther down we saw six burial scaffolds, and on the ground beneath them were the bones of as many Indians, the skull of one of them having been pierced by and still containing a rifle bullet.

It was nearly dark when we reached the lower ford, about half-way through the abandoned Indian village, where we camped for the night, wet, cold, hungry and greatly fatigued.

Supper was quickly prepared, and after eating and taking a short smoke, we spread our wet blankets on the ground, and all turned in for the night; but not to sleep, for coyotes and wolves kept up their horrid din, as though angry at being deprived of their accustomed nightly hunt for scraps of muscle and flesh on bones scattered about.

We had been lying down some time, when a yell rent the air, and Jack Healey sprang to his feet shouting "snakes!"

Jack, while nearly asleep, had felt a cold, slimy something crawl over his face, and then followed the warning cry of "snakes!"

We were soon on our feet, quickly replenished the dying fire, and with sabres in hand began to hunt for the unwelcome intruders. No snakes were found, but we found lizards, hundreds of the slimy green things, and the slaughter continued until the last one found was dead. Then we tried our blankets again but dread of another attack by the repulsive things did not allow us to fall asleep. Soon another man felt one of the reptiles crawling over him, and then all arose and there was another slaughter of lizards. Sleep was out of the question. So we lay and sat around until morning dawned.

After a hasty breakfast we passed on over the battlefield, where a little over one year ago, General George A. Custer and three hundred brave troopers of the Seventh Cavalry, while in the line of duty, were massacred by between three and four thousand Indian warriors under the immediate command of Sitting Bull. Not one of the hostiles having part in that massacre has ever been called to account for the awful deed. Worse than that, some of these very same savages, are now fed and supported by the government they fought against, and are the forced associates and companions of members of the Seventh Cavalry!

The bodies of our dead had never been properly buried. All these months had passed, yet the little band whose brave deeds of heroism will ever remain a matter of history, have not received decent burial. Their bones, divested of clothing by the heartless and brutal savages, and of flesh by wolves and other animals, lie bleaching on the ground where they fell, a said result

151

of the failure of Major Reno to give expected support.

Two days after the battle a small detachment was sent to bury the bodies, but not one was given proper interment—graves were shallow, and dirt thrown but sparsely over bodies was soon washed away by rains or dug away by scavenger animals and birds.

Crossing the Little Horn, or Custer River as it is now called, to the east side, a well-defined trail leads up the gradual slope a quarter of a mile in length. The ground is covered with sage brush, coarse grass, prickly pears, and is destitute of rocks or timber. We reach the summit, and see a ravine with gentle sloping sides, near a half-mile in length—and free from rocks, timber, or anything that could furnish shelter. Nearby are the uncovered remains of eighteen men, in six piles, with a piece of *tepee* pole sticking in the ground at each pile.

Upon one of these "tombstones" hung a white *sombrero*, relic of a member of the Seventh Cavalry, with two bullet holes through it, and a long cut as if made with an axe; and nearby we found an axe, with a dark stain on the rusty blade, it having undoubtedly been used by the squaws in their frenzied mutilation of the wounded and dead of the Curtis command. Near here were the carcasses of two horses; to the north, a few yards away, were heaps of bones so mixed that it was not possible to count the number of persons represented, A little farther on, and another heap containing the bones of three men appear beside the skeleton of a horse, evidently killed to be used as a breastwork.

A heavy trail runs along the crest of the divide, which separates the river from the ravine, and it was thickly strewn with whitened bones, rotting equipments and clothing.

Three hundred yards up the trail, we came upon the knoll where Custer and the remnant of his command made their final stand. We picture him in our mind, as he coolly loads and fires with the rest of the men, frequently glancing over the bluffs to see if Reno, whom he had so urgently requested to hasten to his support, is at hand. Reno's utter failure to respond is generally condemned.

This elevation of the battlefield is but a little above the divide of which it is the terminus, and is, apparently, a commanding position. But the enemy were too powerful for the small body of troops who were there. On top of the hill where Custer was killed, we saw the skeletons of four men and horses, among the latter being the skeleton of the horse that Custer rode.

We return to Tongue River, with the picture of that field of death vividly impressed on our mind, and wondering if Custer and is men would have perished had Reno tried to fight his way to Custer's rescue. Trumpeter Martin says Reno could have got there; and Trumpeter Martin knows, as he is the man Custer sent back to ask Reno to hurry to his assistance.

CHAPTER THIRTY-FOUR

Back Home!

At the Fort Rice army hospital, our bunch of victims of the final stand of Chief Joseph, passed the fall and part of the winter, while there was a gradual thinning out.

Some were discharged, others returned to quarters, and still others returned to duty, and yet there were eighteen of us in the ward, but all considered out of danger by Surgeon Taylor.

I was one day called to the office of the commanding officer, and as I entered, Colonel Otis looked up, and in his gruff voice asked me if I wanted to go to the Soldiers' Home at Washington. (Otis had taken "sick leave," on furlough, while the chase to overtake Chief Joseph was on, and returned under escort to Fort Rice.)

To his question I answered, "No, sir!"

Otis then informed me that I was to be discharged by reason of Surgeon Taylor's report that I was incurable; and that I could go home, if I had one, or to the Regular Army Soldiers' Home, either one I chose.

His manner was gruff and anything but courteous—he ran true to form—the only name by which he was known among the men under his command when he was in charge of a battalion under Sturges "wandering through the wilderness"—"The Bulldozer!"

I told Otis I thought I could die as well in one place as another, and that I would go to what would be my home. He said "All right," and I returned to the hospital, feeling rather blue.

Here I was, not twenty-four years of age, and to be discharged as incurable!

Well, this meant

No longer to indulge in those long and tiresome marches!

No longer Drill! Drill! Drill!

No more hard-tack and bacon!

Incurable!

I would now have all I could do to keep up on crutches.

Not a very pleasant outlook for a young man, but no use murmuring. No use worrying. Lots of men 'have gone home dead, and I can wiggle! But I did feel all out whack.

In a few days the steward returned from the adjutant's office with his morning report, and coming up to me as I sat on the edge of my cot, held out his hand and said: "Old man, I wish that I was you! You are now your own boss, and will not have to do dog's duty anymore!" And then he handed me a long envelope.

I looked at the address on the outside. It read:

"Mr, A. R Muford, Hospital"

"Well," says I, "there must be something in it, if they address me as 'Mr.' after so many other names."

I opened the envelope and on the inside found a sheet of sheepskin, and on this piece of parchment, filled in with Clerk Hall's best fist, were the following words:—

ARMY OF THE UNITED STATES

To whom it may concern:—

Know ye, that Ami F. Mulford, a trumpeter of Captain T. H. French's Company "M," of the Seventh (7) Regiment of Cavalry, who was enlisted the Fifth day of September, one thousand eight hundred and seventy-six, to serve five years, is hereby discharged from the service of the United States in consequence of Surgeon's Certificate of Disability.

Said Ami F. Mulford was born in Murdston, County—[*this is a clerical error, it should read, Thurston, Steuben County*]- in the State of New York, is 23 7/12 years of age, five feet five inches high, light complexion, blue eyes, light hair, and by occupation when enlisted, a clerk.

Given under my hand at Fort Rice, D.T., this eighteenth day of December, in the year of our Lord one thousand eight hundred and seventy-seven.

[Signed,]   Elmer Otis,
                         Lt.-Col. 7th Cav. Commanding.

Character—Excellent.

[Signed,]   E. G. Mathey,
                                 Captain 7th Cavalry,
                         Commanding Detachment.

I was no longer a soldier.

I am a citizen, and as such as good as any other man, and my own boss; I can now live or die, get fat or starve to death, and it will be nobody's business.

Free, independent—yet crippled for life.

In a few days I received my final statement, had it cashed, and with nearly two hundred dollars in an inside pocket, and my left leg in a sling, to keep it from dragging on the ground, I take my crutches, hobble to the door, and am helped aboard the stage that is to take me to Bismarck, bid goodbye to comrades, and with a last long look at Fort Rice, I start for God's country!

CHAPTER THIRTY-FIVE

A Century of Indian Uprisings Ends

The native occupants of North America, had the entire continent distributed or parcelled out, among the various tribes, so that each knew the metes and bounds of their own territory, and understood that to venture onto the territory of another tribe was to trespass—that meant war. The various Indian tribes had down through the ages worked out the practical adjustment of their physical requirements so that Mother Earth provided for all.

The lesser tribes in some instances formed federations, for mutual protection against invasions by stronger bodies of Indians—as did the Iroquois tribes of New York and North-western Pennsylvania—the Mohawks, Oneidas, Onondagas, Cayugas and Senecas. The Iroquois Federation was formed about 1550. In numbers the Senecas were far in the lead. The Council House of the Iroquois Federation—as at Onondaga Lake; that of the Senecas at Seneca Castle, at the foot of Seneca Lake Each of the affiliated tribes had a Council of its own, and also had equal representation at the Federation Council Fire at Onondaga Lake.

A similar federation, composed of twelve tribes, about half the total being Tuscarora Indians, flourished in North Carolina, until they got into trouble with encroaching whites about 1710, and were defeated in a number of battles. In 1712 the Tuscaroras, being of Iroquois blood, were admitted to membership in the Iroquois Federation before that known as the Five Nations, thence on termed the Six Nations. But so nicely had

the land of the Federation been adjusted to meet the requirements of the original five tribes—or nations—that no territory
was allotted to the Tuscaroras as a tribe, but the members were
distributed among the Oneidas, Onondagas, Senecas, Cayugas
and Mohawks. Tuscaroras had no voice in the Councils of the
Federation.

The immediate purpose of the Iroquois in forming their
Federation was to stop invasions of their lands by the Hurons
and other powerful tribes of the North and Northwest. In 1612
the Seneca country was invaded from the north by a French
army, bent on conquest, accompanied by a large number of Hu-
ron warriors. The Senecas stood their ground and repulsed the
invaders, inflicting great loss. The French soldiers were armed
with guns; the Senecas with bows and arrows, spears, war clubs,
stone tomahawks and darts thrown with throngs fastened to
sticks.

The Indians had no written language. Property in the various tribes was held in common. The religious instinct found
expression in many ways, in the legends and activities of all the
American Indians. They believed in a Great Spirit, supreme over
all, the source of their being; also in beneficent spirits of less
degree, and in evil spirits who caused afflictions and disasters.
To the mind of an Indian, everything he came in contact with,
whether animate or inanimate, possessed spirit life and magic
power. The paramount idea of their Faith, was a Happy Hunting
Ground, of boundless extent, above the skies; a land of eternal
summer, of peace and plenty.

When charters were granted the colonies of Massachusetts
and of Connecticut, the grants covered territory extending entirely across the continent from the Atlantic Ocean to the Pacific
Ocean!

Those who fled from Old World oppressions, and colonized
the Atlantic sea board, did not consider that the Indians had
rights that should be respected.

Every effort on the part of the natives, to hold or regain
possession of land taken, by force or artifice, from them by the

invading whites, but hastened the inevitable end.

At a Treaty held in July, 1755, called by Sir William Johnson, representing the English government, with a view to adjusting troubles due to encroachments by whites on hunting grounds along the Susquehanna River, the chief spokesman of the Six Nations said:—

> Brother:You desire us to unite and live together, and draw all our allies near us, but we shall have no land left, either for ourselves or them, for your people when they buy a small piece of land of us, by stealing they make it large.We desire such things may not be done, and that your people may not be suffered to buy any more of our land.

The encroachments of the whites on the lands of the Indians, have been unyielding and persistent, and the so-called Frontier, extending from the northern to the southern bounds of this government, was pushed westward from the Atlantic Ocean, until it was met in the far west by a frontier line moving eastward from the Pacific Ocean, and then came the final battle between United States troops, under General Miles, and the Nez Perces' warriors in the Bad-Lands of the Great Northwest, where the curtain was finally rung down, when Chief Joseph surrendered to General Miles, October 5th, 1877.

www.ingramcontent.com/pod-product-compliance
Lightning Source LLC
Chambersburg PA
CBHW021110090426
42738CB00006B/585